Study Guide and Practice Workbook

Mathematics

Applications and Connections

Course 2

Glencoe
McGraw-Hill

New York, New York   Columbus, Ohio   Woodland Hills, California   Peoria, Illinois

Glencoe/McGraw-Hill

A Division of The McGraw·Hill Companies

Send all inquiries to:
Glencoe/McGraw-Hill
936 Eastwind Drive
Westerville, OH 43081-3374

ISBN: 0-02-833124-9   *Study Guide and Practice Workbook, Course 2*

6 7 8 9 10 066 05 04 03 02 01 00 99

Contents

1-1 Study Guide

A Plan for Problem Solving

In 1966 the average salary for a major league baseball player was $22,500. By 1990 it was over $1,000,000. How many times the 1966 salary is the 1990 salary?

Explore	What is given?	1966 average salary = $22,500
		1990 average salary = over $1,000,000
	What is asked?	How many times the 1966 salary is the 1990 salary?

Plan To find the number of times one number is of another, you need to divide.

Solve

1990 average	divided by	1966 average	is about	times as great
1,000,000	÷	22,500	≈	44.44

The 1990 average salary is about 44 times the 1966 average salary.

Examine You can use multiplication to check division.

$$44.44 \times 22{,}500 \text{ is about } 1{,}000{,}000.$$

So 44.44 is correct.

Use the four-step plan to solve each problem.

1. Kings Canyon National Park is 462 thousand acres. Yellowstone National Park is 2,220 thousand acres. About how many times as large as Kings Canyon is Yellowstone?

2. The flight of Apollo 7 in 1968 was 260 hours and 8 minutes long. The flight of Apollo 17 in 1972 was 301 hours and 52 minutes long. How much longer was the Apollo 17 flight?

3. The Snake River, which runs from Wyoming to Washington, is 1,038 miles long. The Yukon River, which runs from the Yukon territory in Canada to Alaska, is 1,979 miles long. How much longer than the Snake River is the Yukon River?

4. It is 536 miles from Buffalo, New York, to Chicago, Illinois. It is 695 miles from Chicago to Washington, D.C. It is 386 miles from Washington, D.C. to Buffalo. How many miles is it from Buffalo to Chicago to Washington and back to Buffalo?

1-1 **Practice**

A Plan for Problem Solving

Use the four-step plan to solve each problem.

1. **Sports** "Go Dogs, Go Dogs, Go, Go, Go!" is a cheer for the Bulldogs' basketball team. If 15 cheerleaders yell the cheer 5 times, how many times is "Go" said?

   Explore:

   Plan:

   Solve:

   Examine:

2. **Cooking** A can of orange juice concentrate holds 12 ounces. If you mix it with 3 cans of water, how big a pitcher do you need to hold it all?

   Explore:

   Plan:

   Solve:

   Examine:

1-2 Study Guide

Order of Operations

Algebraic expressions are evaluated using these rules.

Order of Operations
1. Do all operations within grouping symbols first.
2. Multiply and divide in order from left to right.
3. Add and subtract in order from left to right.

Example   Evaluate $56 \div (17 - 9) + 7 \times 3$.

$$
\begin{aligned}
56 \div (17 - 9) + 7 \times 3 &= 56 \div 8 + 7 \times 3 \qquad && \textit{Subtract 9 from 17.} \\
&= \quad 7 \quad + 7 \times 3 && \textit{Divide 56 by 8.} \\
&= \quad 7 \quad + \quad 21 && \textit{Multiply 7 and 3.} \\
&= 28 && \textit{Add 7 and 21.}
\end{aligned}
$$

Name the operation that should be done first in each expression.

1. $(9 + 3) \times 7$

2. $98 - 5 \times 7$

3. $5 \times (9 - 1)$

4. $(15 \div 3) + (4 + 5)$

5. $5 \times 4 \div 2$

6. $5(5 - 3) \times 2$

Evaluate each expression.

7. $2 \times 9 + 5 \times 3$

8. $(9 - 4) \div 5$

9. $10 - 4 + 1$

10. $15 - 18 \div 9 + 3$

11. $30 \div (12 - 6) + 4$

12. $(72 - 12) \div 2$

13. $2(16 - 9) - (5 + 1)$

14. $(43 - 23) - 2 \times 5$

15. $90 - 45 - 24 \div 2$

16. $81 \div (13 - 4)$

17. $7 \times 8 - 2 \times 8$

18. $71 + (34 - 34)$

1-2 Practice

Order of Operations

Name the operation that should be done first in each expression.

1. $5 + 4 \cdot 7$ **2.** $13(6 + 3)$ **3.** $(4 - 2) + 6$

4. $6 \times 8 \div 4$ **5.** $32 \div 4 \times 2$ **6.** $9(4 + 2) \div 3$

Evaluate each expression.

7. $8 \cdot 7 + 8 \cdot 3$ **8.** $(9 - 3) \div 3$

9. $8 - 6 + 3$ **10.** $18 \div 3 \cdot 6$

11. $9 - 4 \div 2 + 6$ **12.** $24 \div (6 - 2)$

13. $18 - (7 - 7)$ **14.** $32 \div (8 - 4)$

15. $90 - 16 \div 4$ **16.** $3(18 - 12) - (5 - 3)$

17. $(24 - 10) - 3 \times 3$ **18.** $4(22 - 18) - 3 \cdot 5$

19. $12(5 - 5) + 3 \cdot 5$ **20.** $18(4 - 3) \div 3 + 3$

21. $(34 + 46) \div 20 + 20$ **22.** $92 - 66 - 12 \div 4$

23. $9 \cdot 3 + 8 \div 4$ **24.** $9 + (18 \div 3)$

Insert parentheses to make each sentence true.

25. $32 + 8 \times 3 \div 4 = 30$ **26.** $15 - 3 \div 1 \cdot 6 = 2$

27. $\frac{88}{22} + 8 \div 3 = 4$ **28.** $18 \div 3 + 3 - 2 = 1$

28. $16 - 8 \div 4 + 10 = 12$ **30.** $5 \cdot 5 + 5 - 5 = 45$

31. $6 + 6 \div 6 \cdot 6 = 42$ **32.** $200 - 90 + 80 + 20 = 10$

1-3 Study Guide

Integration: Algebra
Variables and Expressions

The area of a triangle can be found by multiplying the base of the triangle by the height of the triangle and then dividing by 2.

If we use b to represent the base of the triangle and h to represent the height of the triangle, the area of the triangle can be found by evaluating the **algebraic expression** below.

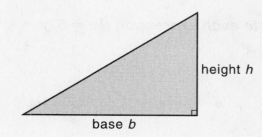

height h

base b

$$\frac{bh}{2}$$

The values of b and h change for different triangles. They are called **variables.**

Examples   **Find the area of each triangle.**

Triangle A:
Evaluate $\frac{bh}{2}$
if $b = 6$
and $h = 7$.

$$\frac{6 \times 7}{2} = \frac{42}{2}$$

$$= 21$$

7

6

The area is 21 square units.

Triangle B:
Evaluate $\frac{bh}{2}$
if $b = 8$
and $h = 10$.

$$\frac{8 \times 10}{2} = \frac{80}{2}$$

$$= 40$$

10

8

The area is 40 square units.

Evaluate each expression if $a = 2$, $b = 3$, $c = 4$, and $d = 12$.

1. $c + 2a$

2. $19 - d$

3. $3(b + 5)$

4. $bc \div 12$

5. $d - c + 6$

6. $a(d - b)$

7. $15 - ab$

8. $6ca$

9. $6 + \frac{d}{c}$

10. $\frac{d}{a} - b$

11. $20 - \frac{2b}{a}$

12. $6c - 4b$

13. $7ab$

14. $a(6 + c) + 1$

15. $2c + 2b - d$

16. $d + ac$

Practice

Integration: Algebra
Variables and Expressions

Evaluate each expression if x = 5, y = 4, and z = 3.

1. $x + 3$

2. $z - 3$

3. $10 - z$

4. $13 + y$

5. $x + z$

6. $y + z$

7. $y + 3 - z$

8. $x - 2 + z$

9. $x - x + 4$

10. $x - y + 8$

11. $xy - 2$

12. $xz - 4$

13. $yz + 10$

14. $yz - 10$

15. $xz + 4$

Evaluate each expression if a = 8, b = 4, and c = 2.

16. $a + b + c$

17. $4b + a$

18. $cb - a$

19. $\frac{a}{b} + 5$

20. $3bc$

21. $\frac{a}{b} + c$

22. $\frac{2a}{4} - b$

23. $3(b + a) - c$

24. $2b - 3c$

25. $\frac{2b}{c}$

26. $\frac{6(a + c)}{b}$

27. $b(b + a) - b$

Evaluate each expression if a = 12, b = 3, c = 4, m = 9, and n = 3.

28. $\frac{m}{n} + 6$

28. $1mn$

30. $\frac{a}{c} - b$

31. $\frac{3n}{m} + 4$

32. $3(n + n) - m$

33. $4c - 3b$

34. $10 - \frac{2m}{n}$

35. $\frac{3(b + c)}{(b + c)}$

36. $b(c - b) + c$

1-4 Study Guide

Integration: Algebra
Powers and Exponents

A **power** can be used to show repeated multiplication of a number.

4×4 can be written 4^2. This is read *4 squared* or *4 to the second power*.

The exponent, 2, tells you how many times
the base, 4, is used as a factor.

base $\longrightarrow 4^2 \longleftarrow$ exponent

Examples **1** **Write $6 \times 6 \times 6 \times 6$ using exponents.**

The base, 6, is used as a factor 4 times. So, $6 \times 6 \times 6 \times 6 = 6^4$.

2 **Write 12^3 as a product.**

The exponent 3 means that 12 is used as a factor 3 times.
$12^3 = 12 \times 12 \times 12$

3 **Evaluate 6^4.**

$6 \times 6 \times 6 \times 6 = 1,296$

Write each power as a product of the same factor.

1. 7^4

2. 5^5

3. 4^6

4. 8^2

5. 9^3

6. 6^1

7. 2^5

8. m^4

Write each product using exponents.

9. $5 \times 5 \times 5$

10. 10×10

11. $6 \times 6 \times 6 \times 6 \times 6$

12. $3 \times 3 \times 3 \times 3$

Evaluate each expression.

13. 8^2

14. 1^6

15. 3^4

16. 12^1

17. 2^5

18. 5^3

19. 4^4

20. 6^2

1-4 Practice

Integration: Algebra
Powers and Exponents

Write each power as a product of the same factor.

1. 5^4

2. 3^5

3. 8^4

4. 15^4

5. 6^7

6. n^4

Write each product using exponents.

7. $8 \cdot 8 \cdot 8$

8. $12 \cdot 12 \cdot 12 \cdot 12 \cdot 12 \cdot 12$

9. $m \cdot m \cdot m \cdot m$

10. $3 \cdot 3 \cdot 3$

11. $1 \cdot 1 \cdot 1 \cdot 1 \cdot 1$

12. $r \cdot r \cdot r \cdot r \cdot r \cdot r$

Evaluate each expression.

13. 3^2

14. 3^3

15. 2^5

16. 0^6

17. 12 squared

18. 3 to the fourth power

19. In 1980, the federal government spent about 2×10^9 dollars on school lunches. In 1995, the amount was up to about 4×10^9 dollars. How much did the government spend on school lunches in 1995?

Use a calculator to determine whether each sentence is true or false.

20. $4^5 > 5^4$

21. $6^5 = 5^8$

22. $5^4 = 10^2$

Evaluate each expression.

23. y^2 if $y = 9$

24. m^6 if $m = 3$

25. x^5 if $x = 10$

26. z^4 if $z = 6$

27. x^3 if $x = 6$

28. y^5 if $y = 7$

1-5 **Study Guide**

Integration: Algebra
Solving Equations

An equation is a mathematical sentence that contains an equals sign.

Example   **Phil can address 50 envelopes in an hour. How long will it take him to address 300 envelopes?**

Let h represent the number of hours. The problem can be represented by $50 \times h = 300$.

$50 \times h = 300$
$50 \times 6 \overset{?}{=} 300$
You know that $50 \times 6 = 300$.
The solution is 6.

It will take Phil 6 hours to address 300 envelopes.

Name the number that is a solution of the given equation.

1. $r - 12 = 20$; 8, 24, 32

2. $10m = 80$; 8, 10, 70

3. $k + 25 = 50$; 15, 25, 75

4. $y \div 9 = 8$; 64, 72, 80

5. $6p = 72$; 8, 10, 12

6. $48 - n = 12$; 32, 36, 60

Solve each equation.

7. $x + 22 = 66$

8. $t - 17 = 23$

9. $12f = 144$

10. $\frac{\ell}{7} = 10$

11. $25w = 225$

12. $176 - 45 = b$

13. $19 \times s = 171$

14. $210 \div v = 14$

Mathematics: Applications and Connections, Course 2

1-5 Practice

Integration: Algebra
Solving Equations

Name the number that is a solution of the given equation.

1. $y + 12 = 16$ 4, 5, 6

2. $m - 15 = 23$ 8, 38, 18

3. $12x = 72$ 6, 7, 8

4. $n \div 10 = 11$ 9, 100, 110

5. $44 + s = 92$ 48, 58, 52

6. $15 \times 8 = r$ 40, 80, 120

7. $z \div 11 = 9$ 20, 90, 99

8. $32 - 16 = t$ 6, 16, 24

Solve each equation.

9. $x + 42 = 83$

10. $w - 13 = 77$

11. $x + 5 = 22$

12. $q - 12 = 44$

13. $5m = 35$

14. $u \div 10 = 100$

15. $25v = 650$

16. $14x = 154$

17. $\frac{84}{m} = 7$

18. $\frac{y}{10} = 67$

19. $q - 92 = 138$

20. $p \div 12 = 9$

21. A number plus 7 is 12. What is the number? Use the equation $x + 7 = 12$.

22. The quotient of a number and 19 is 6. Find the number. Use the equation $\frac{y}{19} = 6$.

23. Consider the equation $1 \cdot x = y$. What can you say about x and y?

Name_____ Date_____

1-6 Study Guide

Integration: Geometry
Fractals and Other Patterns

A **fractal** is a geometric figure that is made up of smaller replicas of the entire shape repeated over and over again in different sizes. Note how the pattern continues for the fractal below.

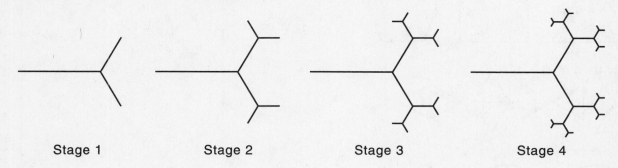

Stage 1   Stage 2   Stage 3   Stage 4

Draw the next two figures that continue each pattern.

1.

2.

3.

4.

5.

6

Mathematics: Applications and Connections, Course 2

1-6 Practice

Integration: Geometry
Fractals and Other Patterns

Draw the next two figures that continue each pattern.

1.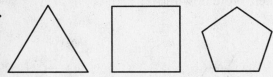

2.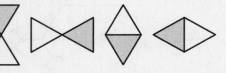

3.

4.

5.

6.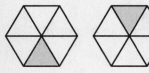

7.

1-7 Study Guide

Integration: Geometry
Area

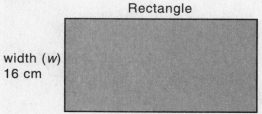

Rectangle

width (*w*) 16 cm

length (ℓ) 40 cm

The area of a rectangle equals the product of its length and its width.

$A = \ell w$
$A = 40 \cdot 16$
$A = 640 \text{ cm}^2$

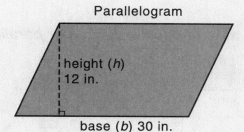

Parallelogram

height (*h*) 12 in.

base (*b*) 30 in.

The area of a parallelogram equals the product of its base and its height.

$A = bh$
$A = 30 \cdot 12$
$A = 360 \text{ in}^2$

Find the area of each rectangle or parallelogram.

1.

6 cm

14 cm

2.

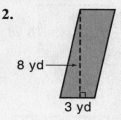

8 yd

3 yd

3.

7 mm

12 mm

4.

2 in.

8 in.

5.

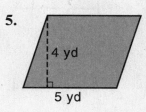

4 yd

5 yd

6.

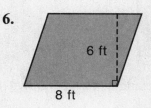

6 ft

8 ft

7. parallelogram: $b = 15$ ft, $h = 21$ ft

8. rectangle: $\ell = 8$ cm, $w = 12$ cm

9. parallelogram: $b = 5$ m, $h = 2$ m

10. rectangle: $\ell = 100$ yd, $w = 50$ yd

Mathematics: Applications and Connections, Course 2

1-7 Practice

Integration: Geometry
Area

Find the area of each rectangle or parallelogram.

1.
5 in.
13 in.

2.
9 m
2 m

3.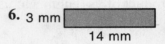
2 ft
10 ft

4.
3 ft
3 ft

5.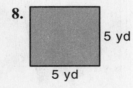
3 ft
9 ft

6.
3 mm
14 mm

7. 4 ft
1 ft

8.
5 yd
5 yd

9.
17 in.
8 in.

10.
3 ft
1 ft

11.
18 cm
42 cm

12.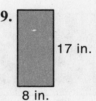
10 yd
10 yd

13. rectangle: $\ell = 2$ in., $w = 8$ in.

14. parallelogram: $b = 24$ ft, $h = 7$ ft

15. parallelogram: $b = 2$ yd, $h = 10$ yd

16. rectangle: $\ell = 18$ mm, $w = 12$ mm

17. rectangle: $\ell = 4$ ft, $w = 2$ ft

18. parallelogram: $b = 2$ ft, $h = 5$ ft

19. What is the length of a rectangle whose area is 84 in² and whose width is 7 inches?

20. Find the height of a parallelogram with a base of 12 yards and an area of 38 yd².

2-1 Study Guide

Comparing and Ordering Decimals

Which is greater, 36.74 or 36.704?

You can compare decimals like 36.74 and 36.704 on a number line.
Numbers to the right are greater than numbers to the left.

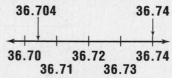

You can also compare decimals by comparing the digits in each
place-value position.

Find the first place in which the digits are different.	Compare the digits.	The decimal with the greater digit is greater.
36.70**4**	0 is less than 4.	36.704 < 36.74
36.74	0 < 4	

Draw a number line to show which decimal is greater.

1. 0.39, 0.35

2. 1.95, 2.02

3. 6.55, 6.50

Replace each ◯ with <, >, or = to make a true sentence.

4. 8.05 ◯ 8.5

5. 0.76 ◯ 0.67

6. 18.20 ◯ 18.2

7. 7.004 ◯ 7.044

8. 6.79 ◯ 6.8

9. 29.922 ◯ 29.299

Order each set of numbers from least to greatest.

10. 0.067, 0.6, 0.76, 0.07

11. 56.2, 55.6, 52.2, 56.02

12. 600.09, 609.06, 600.9, 609.9

13. 0.88, 0.9, 0.08, 0.89

2-1 Practice

Comparing and Ordering Decimals

Use a number line to show which decimal is greater.

1. 0.27, 0.29

2. 1.3, 1.03

3. 1.02, 0.98

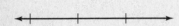

4. 4.42, 4.47

5. 1.305, 1.042

6. 6.12, 6.1

Replace each ◯ with <, >, or = to make a true sentence.

7. 6.02 ◯ 6.01

8. 0.39 ◯ 0.41

9. 6 ◯ 0.6

10. 0.43 ◯ 0.34

11. 0.72 ◯ 0.72

12. 0.0021 ◯ 0.021

13. 0.34 ◯ 0.48

14. 5.2 ◯ 5

15. 3.7 ◯ 3.7

16. 1.47 ◯ 1.47

17. 1.75 ◯ 0.77

18. 4.52 ◯ 0.98

Write a sentence comparing two of the numbers shown on the number line.

19.
```
  0.40   0.60   0.80
```

20.
```
  1.30   1.50   1.70
```

21.
```
  6.1   6.3   6.5
```

Order each set of numbers from least to greatest.

22. 4.03, 4.003, 4.3

23. 0.82, 1.2, 0.92

24. 1.12, 1.135, 1.02

25. 13.72, 1.372, 137.2

26. 6.5, 0.65, 0.065

27. 7.9, 3.46, 9.87, 2.1

8

Name _____ **Date** _____

2-2 Study Guide

Rounding Decimals

Round 24.625 to the nearest tenth.

You can use a number line.

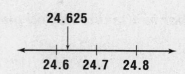

Find the approximate location of 24.625 on the number line.

24.625 is closer to 24.6 than to 24.7.
24.625 rounded to the nearest tenth is 24.6.

You can also round without a number line.

Find the place to which you want to round.	Look at the digit to the right of the place being rounded. The digit remains the same if the digit to the right is 0, 1, 2, 3, or 4. Round up if the digit to the right is 5, 6, 7, 8, or 9.	2 is less than 5. Do not change the digit.
24.**6**25	24.6**2**5	24.6

Round each number to the underlined place-value position.

1. 46.124

2. 29.915

3. 15.1733

4. 0.159

5. 308.862

6. 0.0561

7. 0.577

8. 0.0089

9. 2.62

10. 76.0552

11. 12.1903

12. 0.855

13. 331.98

14. 0.0549

15. 6.03

16. 173.99

17. 84.012

18. 0.846

19. 12.7642

20. 0.062

Mathematics: Applications and Connections, Course 2

2-2 Practice

Rounding Decimals

Round each number to the underlined place-value position.

1. 0.2̲35

2. 3.49̲2

3. 8.076̲9

4. 9̲.4

5. 17.14̲5

6. 0.3̲92

7. 19.32̲08

8. 0.006̲3

9. 16.7̲42

10. 6.1398̲2

11. 0.33̲6

12. 1.87̲3

13. 0.8̲92

14. 0.44̲4

15. 67.9̲03

16. 84̲.590

17. 5.129̲806

18. 9̲9.105

19. 6̲2.017

20. 0.1̲29866

21. 3̲7.09

22. Draw a number line to show that, when rounded to the nearest whole number, 9.8 rounds to 10.

23. The Sears Tower, once the world's tallest building, is 1,454 feet tall. Round this height to the nearest 100 feet.

24. In 1990, the population of St. Louis, Missouri, was 396,685. Round this number to the nearest ten thousand and to the nearest hundred thousand. How do the numbers compare?

2-3 Study Guide

Estimating with Decimals

One way to estimate is by rounding to the greatest place-value position.

Example 1

$$73.2 \times 9.6 \longrightarrow \begin{array}{r} 70 \\ \times 10 \\ \hline 700 \end{array}$$

Estimate a division problem by rounding the divisor. Then round the dividend to a multiple of the divisor.

Example 2

$$72.8 \div 8.9 \longrightarrow 72.8 \div 9$$
$$72 \div 9 = 8$$

Use clustering to estimate sums if the numbers group around a common quantity.

Example 3 $19.3 + 22.4 + 20.9 + 18.6 + 21.2 + 19.1 + 20.5 + 18.9$

All 8 numbers are clustered around 20. The sum is about 20×8 or 160.

Estimate. Use an appropriate strategy.

1. $\begin{array}{r} 32.19 \\ 29.36 \\ 30.08 \\ 28.9 \\ + 31.0 \\ \hline \end{array}$

2. $\begin{array}{r} 5.6 \\ \times 2.1 \\ \hline \end{array}$

3. $\begin{array}{r} 16.7 \\ - 12.2 \\ \hline \end{array}$

4. $\begin{array}{r} 93.5 \\ 22.1 \\ 49.9 \\ + 18.8 \\ \hline \end{array}$

5. $61.9 \div 7.1$

6. 8.8×2.1

7. $41.2 \div 5.9$

8. $56.82 - 21.12$

9. $\begin{array}{r} \$3.92 \\ + 4.18 \\ \hline \end{array}$

10. $\begin{array}{r} 49.7 \\ \times 30.5 \\ \hline \end{array}$

11. $\begin{array}{r} 9.74 \\ \times 4.08 \\ \hline \end{array}$

12. $\begin{array}{r} \$41.15 \\ - 19.09 \\ \hline \end{array}$

13. $878 \div 8$

14. $\begin{array}{r} 18.6 \\ \times 2.4 \\ \hline \end{array}$

15. $97.7 \div 9.8$

16. $\begin{array}{r} \$45.92 \\ - 33.35 \\ \hline \end{array}$

2-3 Practice

Estimating with Decimals

Estimate by rounding.

1.   5.98
   $+9.82$

2.   8.2
   $\times 9.1$

3. $6.8\overline{)49.42}$

4. $7.2\overline{)84.1}$

5. $29.8\overline{)986.24}$

6. $6.3\overline{)89.92}$

Estimate by clustering.

7. $71.1 + 69.8 + 70.9$

8. $6.8 + 7.3 + 7.1$

9. $15.2 + 14.9 + 14.8$

Estimate. Use an appropriate strategy.

10. $9.82
    8.71
   $+6.18$

11.   2.4
   $+8.87$

12.   29.53
   -18.12

13.   8.9
   $\times 6.1$

14.   27.2
   $\times 9.7$

15. $5.3\overline{)39.61}$

16. $3.1 + 2.9 + 2.87 + 3.3$

17. $81.2 + 79.9 + 80.22$

18. $30.2\overline{)119.1}$

2-4

Study Guide

Multiplying Decimals

Multiply decimals just like you multiply whole numbers. The number of decimal places in the product is equal to the sum of the number of decimal places in the factors.

Example   **Multiply 0.038 and 0.17.**

$$
\begin{array}{r}
0.038 \\
\times\ 0.17 \\
\hline
266 \\
38\ \ \\
\hline
0.00646
\end{array}
$$

$\leftarrow$ *three decimal places*
$\leftarrow$ *two decimal places*

$\leftarrow$ *five decimal places*

The product is 0.00646.

Multiply.

1. 0.8
$\times\ 7$

2. 0.04
$\times\ 0.3$

3. 0.16
$\times\ 26$

4. 0.003
$\times\ 4.2$

5. 12.2×0.06

6. 0.0015×0.15

7. 1.9×2.2

8. 3.59×0.02

9. 12.2×0.007

10. 0.7×3.11

Evaluate each expression if m = 0.9 and n = 6.2.

11. $m \times 0.43$

12. $0.002 \times n$

13. $17.4 \times m$

14. $n \times 0.0001$

2-4 Practice

Multiplying Decimals

Place the decimal point in each product.

1. $1.47 \times 6 = 882$ 2. $0.9 \times 2.7 = 243$ 3. $6.48 \times 2.4 = 15552$

Multiply.

4. $\begin{array}{r} 0.6 \\ \times 0.7 \\ \hline \end{array}$
5. $\begin{array}{r} 6.3 \\ \times 5.1 \\ \hline \end{array}$
6. $\begin{array}{r} 18.2 \\ \times 0.51 \\ \hline \end{array}$

7. 0.52×0.03 8. 0.29×29.1 9. 6.1×0.0054

10. 6.8×0.39 11. 3.57×0.09 12. 3.72×8.4

Solve each equation.

13. $t = 0.32 \times 0.05$ 14. $6.4 \times 3.9 = h$ 15. $k = 0.09 \times 2.3$

16. $a = 0.4 \times 9$ 17. $0.23 \times 0.003 = m$ 18. $1.09 \times 6.24 = v$

Evaluate each expression if $a = 0.4$ and $b = 5.8$.

19. $0.48 \cdot a$ 20. $b \cdot 13.8$ 21. $0.003 \cdot a$

22. $1.4 \cdot b$ 23. $3.6 \cdot a$ 24. $24.5 \cdot a$

11 *Mathematics: Applications and Connections, Course 2*

2-5 Study Guide

Powers of Ten

You can find the product of a number and a power of 10 without using a calculator or paper and pencil. Suppose you wanted to find the product of 23.7 and powers of 10.

Decimal		Power of Ten		Product
23.7	×	0.001	=	0.0237
23.7	×	0.01	=	0.237
23.7	×	0.1	=	2.37
23.7	×	10^0 or 1	=	23.7
23.7	×	10^1 or 10	=	237
23.7	×	10^2 or 100	=	2,370
23.7	×	10^3 or 1,000	=	23,700
23.7	×	10^4 or 10,000	=	237,000

For powers of 10 that are greater than 1, the exponent in the power of 10 tells you the number of places to move the decimal point to the right. For powers of 10 that are less than 1, the decimal point moves to the left.

Examples
1 $0.08 \times 10^4 = 800$ *Move the decimal point 4 places to the right.*

2 $6.25 \times 0.001 = 0.00625$ *Move the decimal point 3 places to the left.*

Multiply mentally.

1. 0.8×0.1

2. 6.12×10^2

3. $8.4 \times 1,000$

4. 9.3×0.001

5. 4.006×100

6. 67.8×0.01

Solve each equation.

7. $x = 89 \times 10,000$

8. $2.9 \times 10^3 = n$

9. $y = 24.78 \times 0.01$

10. $0.0004 \times 10^4 = p$

11. $v = 589 \times 0.001$

12. $r = 0.01 \times 10^0$

2-5 Practice

Powers of Ten

Multiply mentally.

1. 15.24×10

2. 2.48×0.1

3. 0.702×100

4. 0.9×0.001

5. $5.149 \times 1,000$

6. 0.52×100

7. 2.587×10^0

8. 0.2674×100

9. 1.5×0.01

10. 6.8×10^2

11. 9.57×10^4

12. 6.2×10^5

Solve each equation.

13. $d = 0.92 \times 100$

14. $12.43 \times 0.01 = h$

15. $h = 3.68 \times 10^6$

16. $a = 0.004 \times 10^2$

17. $0.23 \times 1,000 = j$

18. $1.89 \times 10^0 = v$

19. $2.098 \times 0.1 = b$

20. $s = 2.69 \times 10$

21. $m = 963.2 \times 10^4$

22. $c = 20.18 \times 0.0001$

23. $e = 100 \times 0.4$

24. $f = 1,000 \times 82.9$

2-6 Study Guide

Dividing Decimals

To divide by a decimal, change the divisor to a whole number.

Example   **Find 0.5194 ÷ 0.49.**

$$
\begin{array}{r}
1.06 \\
0.49\overline{)0.51.94} \\
\underline{49} \\
2\,94 \\
\underline{2\,94} \\
0
\end{array}
$$

Change 0.49 to 49.
Move the decimal point two places to the right.

Move the decimal point in the dividend the same number of places to the right.

Divide as with whole numbers.

Without finding or changing each quotient, change each problem so that the divisor is a whole number.

1. 3.4 ÷ 1.1

2. 76.44 ÷ 0.006

3. 0.56 ÷ 0.4

4. 89.45 ÷ 0.908

5. 5.675 ÷ 6.8

6. 0.00864 ÷ 0.012

Divide.

7. 0.9)6.3

8. 0.6)0.540

9. 0.3)129

10. 2.4)0.192

11. 0.44)5.28

12. 0.025)0.04

13. 1.3)780

14. 0.08)0.0012

15. 0.7)5.95

Solve each equation.

16. $y = 0.0528 ÷ 0.06$

17. $16.84 ÷ 0.4 = m$

18. $k = 2.05 ÷ 0.5$

Mathematics: Applications and Connections, Course 2

2-6 Practice

Dividing Decimals

Without finding or changing each quotient, change each problem so that the divisor is a whole number.

1. $0.84 \div 0.2$

2. $1.02 \div 0.3$

3. $3.9 \div 1.3$

4. $13.6 \div 0.003$

5. $1.622 \div 1.4$

6. $0.00025 \div 0.035$

Divide.

7. $0.5\overline{)9.5}$

8. $0.8\overline{)0.048}$

9. $0.4\overline{)82}$

10. $3.5\overline{)2.38}$

11. $0.62\overline{)600.16}$

12. $0.015\overline{)0.06}$

13. $1.4\overline{)121.8}$

14. $8\overline{)0.0092}$

15. $0.38\overline{)760.38}$

Solve each equation.

16. $7.8 \div 2.6 = k$

17. $3.92 \div 0.08 = m$

18. $s = 149.73 \div 0.23$

19. $v = 155 \div 0.1$

20. $c = 1,098 \div 6.1$

21. $3,633.4 \div 3.7 = d$

22. $903.6 \div 25.1 = n$

23. $363.6 \div 5 = r$

24. $2.004 \div 0.2 = b$

25. $w = 84.7 \div 3.85$

26. $165.2 \div 8.26 = t$

27. $29.28 \div 1.22 = s$

2-7

Study Guide

Decimals and Fractions

To express a fraction as a decimal, divide the numerator of the fraction by the denominator.

Example   **1**   **Express $\frac{3}{8}$ as a decimal.**

$$\begin{array}{r} 0.375 \\ 8\overline{)3.000} \end{array} \qquad \frac{3}{8} = 0.375$$

A decimal like 0.375 is a terminating decimal. The decimal equivalents for some fractions are repeating decimals rather than terminating decimals. Use a bar to indicate the digits that repeat.

Examples   **2**   **Express $\frac{5}{12}$ as a decimal.**   **3**   **Express $\frac{13}{33}$ as a decimal.**

$$\begin{array}{r} 0.41666 \\ 12\overline{)5.00000} \end{array} = 0.41\overline{6} \qquad \begin{array}{r} 0.393939\ldots = 0.\overline{39} \\ 33\overline{)13.000000} \end{array}$$

4   **Express $5\frac{2}{5}$ as a decimal.**

$$\begin{array}{r} 0.4 \\ 5\overline{)2.0} \end{array} = 0.4 \qquad 5\frac{2}{5} = 5.4$$

Express each fraction or mixed number as a decimal. If the decimal is a repeating decimal, use bar notation.

1. $\frac{7}{20}$ 2. $\frac{7}{10}$ 3. $\frac{3}{4}$ 4. $\frac{4}{5}$

5. $\frac{9}{50}$ 6. $\frac{1}{99}$ 7. $\frac{7}{11}$ 8. $\frac{1}{2}$

9. $\frac{11}{12}$ 10. $\frac{5}{8}$ 11. $\frac{7}{200}$ 12. $\frac{17}{25}$

2-7 Practice

Decimals and Fractions

Write each repeating decimal using bar notation.

1. $0.4666666\ldots$

2. $0.5833333\ldots$

3. $0.1272727\ldots$

Express each fraction or mixed number as a decimal. If the decimal is a repeating decimal, use bar notation.

4. $\frac{3}{5}$

5. $\frac{19}{20}$

6. $3\frac{4}{5}$

7. $\frac{23}{50}$

8. $1\frac{5}{8}$

9. $\frac{19}{25}$

10. $\frac{46}{180}$

11. $\frac{24}{40}$

12. $\frac{7}{8}$

13. $14\frac{37}{50}$

14. $8\frac{7}{8}$

15. $3\frac{8}{9}$

Replace each $\bigcirc$ with <, >, or = to make a true sentence.

16. $\frac{1}{4} \bigcirc \frac{9}{40}$

17. $11\frac{13}{40} \bigcirc 11\frac{3}{8}$

18. $1\frac{3}{8} \bigcirc 1.375$

19. $\frac{2}{25} \bigcirc \frac{22}{250}$

20. $2.78 \bigcirc 2\frac{39}{50}$

21. $\frac{3}{10} \bigcirc \frac{29}{100}$

Mathematics: Applications and Connections, Course 2

2-8 | Study Guide

Integration: Measurement
The Metric System

The metric system is a base-10 system. The meter is the basic
unit of length. The liter is the basic unit of capacity. The gram is
the basic unit of mass.

Prefix	Meaning	Length	Capacity	Mass
kilo–	1,000	kilometer (km)	kiloliter (kL)	kilogram (kg)
	1	meter (m)	liter (L)	gram (g)
centi–	0.01	centimeter (cm)	centiliter (cL)	centigram (cg)
milli–	0.001	millimeter (mm)	milliliter (mL)	milligram (mg)

You can change units by multiplying or dividing by multiples of 10.

Examples   **1**   1.543 L = _____ mL   **2**   6,724 g = _____ kg

To change from liters   *To change from grams*
to milliliters, multiply by   *to kilograms, divide by*
1,000 since 1 L = 1,000 mL.   *1,000 since 1 kg = 1,000 g.*

1.543 L × 1,000 = 1,543 mL   6,724 g × 1,000 = 6.724 kg

Complete.

1. 0.6 L = _____ mL   2. 89 L = _____ kL

3. 62.4 kg = _____ g   4. 673 mm = _____ cm

5. 9.2 m = _____ cm   6. 55.2 g = _____ kg

7. 20 km = _____ m   8. 0.6 cm = _____ mm

9. 2.2 kL = _____ L   10. 4.5 g = _____ mg

11. 5,900 mL = _____ L   12. 2.5 m = _____ mm

2-8 Practice

Integration: Measurement
The Metric System

Complete.

1. 470 mm = _____ cm   2. 63.5 km = _____ m

3. 612 g = _____ kg   4. 12.8 g = _____ mg

5. 8 L = _____ mL   6. 68.2 kg = _____ g

7. 0.8 L = _____ mL   8. 65 km = _____ m

9. 30 g = _____ kg   10. 368 mL = _____ L

11. 84 cm = _____ mm   12. 15.4 cm = _____ m

13. 43 m = _____ cm   14. 92 kg = _____ g

15. 3 L = _____ mL   16. 24 cm = _____ m

17. 9 m = _____ cm   18. 53 km = _____ m

19. 9.5 kg = _____ g   20. 1.5 L = _____ mL

21. 9,876 g = _____ kg   22. 1.1 m = _____ cm

23. 2.3 mm = _____ cm   24. 6,200 cm = _____ m

25. How many milliliters are in 0.09 liters?

26. How many centimeters are in 9.02 kilometers?

27. How many millimeters are in 4.2 kilometers?

28. How many milligrams are in 0.012 kilograms?

Mathematics: Applications and Connections, Course 2

Name _____ Date _____

2-9 Study Guide

Scientific Notation

A number in scientific notation is written as the product of a number that is at least one but less than 10 and a power of ten.

Example   **Write 254,000,000 in scientific notation.**

2.54000000   *Move the decimal point to get a number between 1 and 10.*

2.54×10^8 *The decimal point was moved 8 places. The exponent is 8.*

Write each number in scientific notation.

1. 760

2. 8,400

3. 17,400

4. 900,000

5. 12,000,000

6. 64

7. 5,130,000

8. 189,000,000,000

9. 91,000

10. 800

11. 114,500

12. 3,060

13. 26,600,000

14. 7,500,000

15. 303

16. 810,000,000

2-9 Practice

Scientific Notation

Write each number in scientific notation.

1. 930

2. 500

3. 3,500

4. 8,500

5. 62,000

6. 125

7. 7,435

8. 698

9. 40,800

10. 900,000

11. 10,075

12. 721,500

13. 7,895,000

14. 58,000

15. 97,021

16. 85,700

17. 174,000,000

18. 220,000

19. 8,200,000

20. 241

21. 48,000,000

22. 29,830

23. 854,000,000

24. 3,142

25. 68,000,000

26. 9,170,000

27. 5,023,000

Mathematics: Applications and Connections, Course 2

Study Guide

Frequency Tables

Members of a seventh-grade class were surveyed to determine when to hold the winter dance. The results are shown at the right. On what date should the dance be held?

Dates Reported			
Dec. 9	Dec. 2	Dec. 9	Dec. 8
Dec. 2	Dec. 9	Dec. 8	Dec. 9
Dec. 9	Dec. 2	Dec. 9	Dec. 1
Dec. 2	Dec. 9	Dec. 9	Dec. 9
Dec. 8	Dec. 2	Dec. 9	Dec. 1
Dec. 2	Dec. 9	Dec. 2	Dec. 2
Dec. 8	Dec. 9		

Explore   What do you know?
You know how each person responded.

What are you trying to find?
You are deciding on what date to hold the dance.

Plan   Make a frequency table.

Solve   The frequency table shows that the greatest number of people want to hold the dance on December 9.

Examine   Since December 9 received the greatest number of votes, the winter dance should be held on December 9.

Date	Tally	Frequency
Dec. 1	II	2
Dec. 2	卌 III	8
Dec. 8	IIII	4
Dec. 9	卌 卌 II	12

Solve.

1. Julia asked 12 people she bicycles with how many miles they rode their bicycles last week. She recorded the data in the table at the right.

   a. What was the greatest distance ridden?

   b. What was the least distance?

   c. What was the range of the distances?

   d. Choose an appropriate scale and interval.

Miles Bicycled			
Dave	47.8	Gloria	56.9
Mary	19.9	Izumi	82.1
Lung	66.7	Monty	36.8
Iris	71.2	Kara	61.0
Cruz	56.0	Toshi	76.4
Leon	45.3	Burt	17.5

2. Twenty-one people were asked to name the state in which they were born. The data are shown below.

   NY TX PA NY NY TX CA
   NY CA CA CA NY PA PA
   NY NY PA NY NY CA TX

   a. Make a frequency table for the data.

   b. In which state were the fewest people surveyed born?

   c. How many of the people surveyed were born in California?

3-1 Practice

Frequency Tables

Find the range for each set of data. Choose an appropriate scale and an interval for a frequency table.

1. 8, 2, 6, 10, 3, 4

2. 10, 15, 0, 13, 13, 17, 5

3. 18, 70, 33, 61, 20, 20, 54

4. 664, 320, 500, 500, 425

5. 1, 5, 9, 12, 12, 4, 7

6. 27, 22, 19, 21, 12, 15, 11

7. 55, 59, 53, 95, 98, 76

8. 400, 1,200, 800, 900, 1,100

Choose an appropriate scale and an interval for each set of data. Then make a frequency table.

9.

Hours of TV Watched on Saturdays by Mrs. Mulrooney's Students				
8	7	3	7	6
8	2	4	4	6
6	12	7	6	8
5	4	6	5	2

10.

Weights of Members of Fox Valley Wrestling Team (pounds)			
100	97	84	98
112	98	96	84
96	100	85	98

Name the scale and interval of each number line.

11.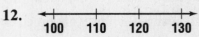
3 6 9 12 15 18 21

12.
100   110   120   130

Mathematics: Applications and Connections, Course 2

3-2

Study Guide

Making Predictions

Graphs can be used to make predictions.

Example   **If the trend in the graph continues, predict about how many records the Sound Store will sell their fifth year in business.**

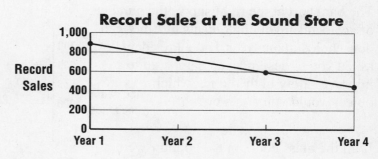

Each year about 150 fewer records have been sold. If the trend continues, the Sound Store will sell about 300 records in the fifth year.

Solve.

1. A store owner is deciding how much of each brand of shampoo to order. She made a graph to show sales for the previous month. Based on the graph, of which brand should she order the most?

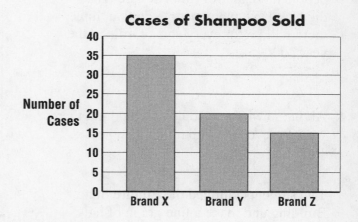

2. Predict the time for the 110-meter hurdles in the 2008 Olympics.

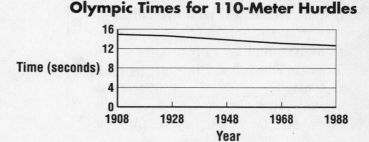

3-2 Practice

Making Predictions

Solve.

1. The bar chart at the right shows the number of accidents involving objects in American households in one year. If the President asked you to design an ad campaign to improve safety in the home, which object would you focus on?

2. If all the glass doors in the country were replaced with unbreakable glass doors, how many fewer accidents do you think there would be next year?

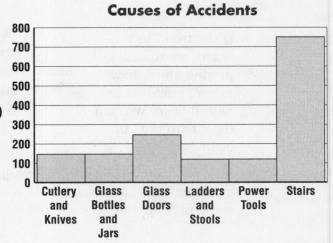

3. The graph at the right shows how many people there are for every square mile in the U.S. How many people do you think there will be for every square mile in the year 2000?

4. About how many people do you think there were for every square mile in the year 1960?

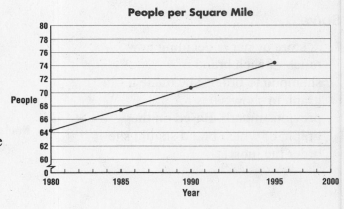

5. Two students climbed the Empire State Building and made a line graph of how far they could see from various heights. About how far do you think they would be able to see from the top of the Eiffel Tower in Paris? It is 301 meters tall.

6. About how far would they see from the top of the KTHI-TV tower in Fargo, North Dakota? The tower is 629 meters tall.

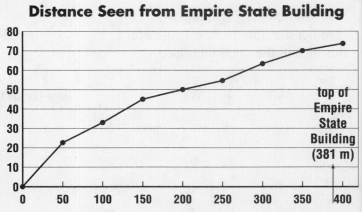

Mathematics: Applications and Connections, Course 2

3-3 Study Guide

Line Plots

Darrell surveyed some kennels to find the cost of grooming his dog. The prices given were: $25.00, $27.00, $32.00, $22.00, $43.00, $28.00, $18.00, $24.00, $25.00, $27.00, $30.00, $24.00, $22.00, $30.00, $12.00, $25.00, and $20.00.

Darrell made a line plot to organize the data on a number line. First he found the range of the data: $43.00 − $12.00 = $31.00. He chose a scale of $10.00 to $45.00 to include all of the data and an interval of $5.00 to separate the data into 7 sections. He drew an × to represent each price. For prices between marked intervals he estimated to position the ×.

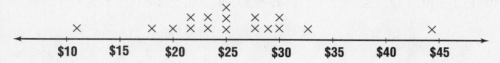

The data are grouped or **clustered** between $20 and $30.

Make a line plot for each set of data.

1. 560, 790, 800, 850, 350, 760, 810, 650, 850, 790, 690, 600

2. 1,750, 2,000, 2,450, 1,900, 1,950, 1,900, 1,900, 1,900, 1,800, 2,100, 2,000, 1,800

3. 7.1, 7.7, 7.8, 8.2, 8.4, 7.5, 7.8, 8.0, 8.3, 8.2, 8.4, 7.6, 8.0

Mathematics: Applications and Connections, Course 2

3-3 Practice

Line Plots

Make a line plot for each set of data.

1. 23, 20, 23, 32, 35, 26, 35, 35, 44

2. 400, 600, 600, 200, 400, 1,000, 400

3. 133, 139, 133, 139, 132, 132, 132, 132

4. 5.3, 5.1, 5.0, 5.0, 6.0, 5.5, 5.3

5. 212, 215, 200, 203, 230, 227, 221, 218, 224

6. $4.30, $4.30, $4.10, $4.30, $4.30, $4.60, $4.10

7. Tom was born in 1958. His brothers and sisters were born in 1950, 1970, 1952, 1955, 1953 and 1956.
  a. Make a line plot for the birth years.

  b. Describe the plot in terms of range and scale.

  c. What have you learned about Tom's family?

Mathematics: Applications and Connections, Course 2

3-4 Study Guide

Mean, Median, and Mode

To find the **mean,** or arithmetic average, of a set of numbers, find the sum of the numbers and divide by the number of items in the set.

To find the **median** of a set of numbers, arrange the numbers in order from least to greatest and find the middle number.

To find the **mode** of a set of numbers, find the number or item that appears most often.

Length of Nine Ladybugs (in inches)		
0.30	0.28	0.34
0.32	0.30	0.31
0.34	0.34	0.30

Example Find the mean, median, and mode of the ladybug lengths.

mean $\dfrac{0.30 + 0.28 + 0.34 + 0.32 + 0.30 + 0.31 + 0.34 + 0.34 + 0.30}{9} \approx 0.31$

mode There are two modes for the data, 0.30 and 0.34.

median 0.28, 0.30, 0.30, 0.30, 0.31, 0.32, 0.34, 0.34, 0.34
$\uparrow$
median

Find the mean, mode(s), and median for each set of data.

1. 6, 3, 7, 1, 8, 4, 8, 9, 4

2. 5.6, 3.2, 7.1, 7.7, 9.0, 6.0, 5.3, 3.2, 4.2

3. 70, 55, 42, 31, 78, 93, 54, 75, 35, 41, 64

4. 2,300, 2,350, 2,240, 2,500, 2,300

5. 21, 56, 34, 27, 42, 21, 77, 41, 77

6. 450, 370, 190, 220, 540, 560, 270, 110, 230

Mathematics: Applications and Connections, Course 2

Mean, Median, and Mode

Find the mean, mode(s), and median for each set of data.

1. 31, 18, 19, 18, 18, 17, 12

2. 5, 0, 9, 9, 3, 0, 5, 5, 4

3. 81, 81, 83, 84, 83, 85, 86

4. 77, 70, 65, 62, 65, 80, 85

5. 5, 6, 3, 9, 0, 4, 1, 2, 7

6. 9, 9, 3, 2, 8, 7, 1, 1, 8

7. 24, 33, 43, 44, 23, 41, 40

8. 77, 76, 55, 76, 66, 58, 55

9. 3.8, 4.2, 4.0, 4.2, 4.2

10. 8.1, 9.0, 9.1, 8.4, 8.4, 8.4, 8.4

11. 1,220, 1,440, 1,220, 1,660, 1,660

12. 3,200, 3,100, 3,100, 3,000, 3,300

Use the table at the right to answer the following.

13. Find the mean, mode(s), and median of the five countries military research and development spending.

14. Find the mean, mode, and median of the countries' civilian research and development spending.

Money spent on Research and Development in Selected Countries (billions of dollars)		
Country	**Military**	**Civilian**
United States	37.3	79.4
United Kingdom	3.5	8.5
France	3.5	14.6
West Germany	1.4	26.1
Japan	0.3	44.0

Mathematics: Applications and Connections, Course 2

Study Guide

Stem-and-Leaf Plots

The table below shows the number of home runs Hank Aaron hit by year.

Home Runs Hit by Hank Aaron

Year	1954	1955	1956	1957	1958	1959	1960	1961	1962	1963	1964	1965
Home Runs	13	27	26	44	30	39	40	35	45	44	24	32
Year	1966	1967	1968	1969	1970	1971	1972	1973	1974	1975	1976	
Home Runs	44	39	29	44	38	47	34	40	20	12	10	

A **stem-and-leaf plot** of the data is shown below.

The tens digits are the *stems*.
The ones digits are the *leaves*.
They are arranged in each row from least to greatest.
4 | 0 means 40.

Stem	Leaf
1	0 2 3
2	0 4 6 7 9
3	0 2 4 5 8 9 9
4	0 0 4 4 4 4 5 7

Make a stem-and-leaf plot for each set of data.

1. 89, 54, 67, 78, 65, 89, 57, 87, 75, 59, 65, 72, 59, 60, 73, 65

2. 85, 124, 90, 113, 107, 94, 88, 114, 106, 109, 110, 117, 100, 101, 119

Refer to the stem-and-leaf plot for Hank Aaron's home runs.

3. What was the greatest number of home runs in a year? What was the fewest home runs in a year?

4. In how many years did Hank Aaron hit 30 or more home runs?

5. What is the mode for the data?

6. What is the median for the data?

3-5 Practice

Stem-and-Leaf Plots

Write the stems that would be used in a stem-and-leaf plot for each set of data.

1. 44, 32, 77, 44, 31, 45, 79, 34, 35, 66, 55

2. 56, 48, 90, 69, 82, 91, 44, 55, 60, 72

3. 5, 3, 33, 58, 22, 39, 40, 38, 22, 57, 29

4. 20, 13, 15, 6, 16, 29, 24, 22, 21, 20, 18, 3, 22

5. 89, 134, 79, 65, 85, 132, 101, 88, 100

6. 94, 68, 90, 35, 84, 92, 103, 88, 91, 80

Make a stem-and-leaf plot for each set of data.

7. 18, 67, 35, 20, 45, 55, 69, 23, 34, 58, 61, 43, 56, 63, 29, 32

8. 82, 91, 80, 105, 113, 104, 83, 90, 84, 91, 109, 112, 100, 92, 85, 92, 92

9. $1.13, $1.25, $1.19, $1.32, $1.25, $1.50, $1.45, $1.48, $1.52, $1.19

10. $0.89, $1.12, $0.92, $1.28, $1.25, $1.02, $1.13, $1.02, $1.01, $1.10, $1.14, $1.23

Use the stem-and-leaf plot to answer the following.

11. How many zero-degree days does the coldest metropolitan area in the United States have in a year?

12. What is the range of the zero-degree day data?

Number of zero-degree days per year in the eight coldest metropolitan areas of the United States:

Stem	Leaf
3	1 3 4 5
4	1
5	1 1 4

3 | 1 = 31 zero-degree days per year

Mathematics: Applications and Connections, Course 2

3-6 Study Guide

Box-and-Whisker Plots

A **box-and-whisker plot** summarizes data using the median, the upper and lower quartiles, and the extreme (highest and lowest) values.

Example   **Draw a box-and-whisker plot to show these data.**
50 53 57 60 65 66 68 70 71 71 71 71 85

On a number line, graph the following points.

lower extreme: 50   upper extreme: 85   median: 68
upper quartile: 71   lower quartile: 58.5

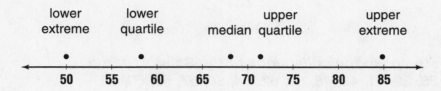

Draw a box around the quartile values.
Draw a vertical line through the median.
Extend whiskers from the quartiles to the upper and lower extremes.

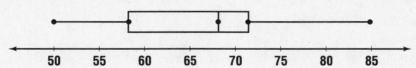

Use the box-and-whisker plot below to answer each question.

1. What is the median?

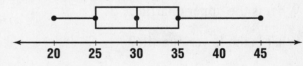

2. What are the upper and lower extremes?

3. What is the interquartile range?

4. Draw a box-and-whisker plot for the data in the stem-and-leaf plot.

Stem	Leaf
3	0 5 6
4	0 2 6 7
5	1 3 8 9 9
6	0 2 4

3/5 = 35

22   *Mathematics: Applications and Connections, Course 2*

3-6 Practice

Box-and-Whisker Plots

Compare the box-and-whisker plots shown at the right.

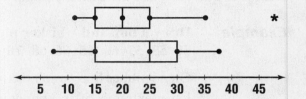

1. What is similar about the data in the two plots?

2. What does the "✳" represent?

3. What is the median of the data in the lower plot?

Number of U.S. stamps in the collections of the School Stamp Club members: 36, 39, 41, 42, 48, 50, 52, 54, 56, 57, 59, 60, 62, 62, 68, 75, 77, 77, 78, 78, 80, 81, 81, 84, and 100.

4. Draw a box-and-whisker plot of the Stamp Club data.

5. What is the range?

6. What is the median?

7. What is the upper quartile?

8. What is the lower quartile?

9. What are the limits on the outlier?

10. Are there any outliers?

11. Draw a box-and-whisker plot from the data shown in the stem-and-leaf plot below.

Stem	Leaf
2	8
3	0 1 1 5 8 9
4	0 0 1 1 1 3 3 4 5 7 8
5	0 2 4 5

5|2 = 52

Mathematics: Applications and Connections, Course 2

3-7 Study Guide

Misleading Statistics

Don't be misled by statistics. Choose the best measure of central tendency to describe the data.

Measure of Central Tendency	When to Use
mean	when no numbers are much greater or much less than the rest
mode	when the most frequently occurring number is needed
median	when there are numbers that are much greater or much less than the rest

Example   A car dealer advertised that the average savings on a new car purchased from her was $1,500.

Number of Sales	Amount of Savings
2	$5,000
1	$3,500
9	$500

The mean of the data in the table is $1,500. The median and the mode are both $500. $500 is more representative of the savings you might expect if you buy a car from this dealer.

The members of a health club compiled the table below. It shows how many laps various swimmers completed.

1. Find the mean, mode, and median of the data.

2. Which measure is least descriptive?

3. Which number most accurately describes the data?

Number of Laps	People
10	9
15	7
20	5
25	10

3-7 Practice

Misleading Statistics

1. A company that sells computer diskettes wants to encourage customers to buy more by showing how much the price drops as you buy more diskettes.

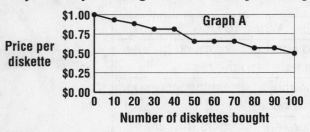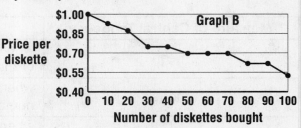

   a. Which graph would they print in their catalog?
   b. How is the graph at the right misleading?

2. Tina weighs herself every month. Her weights for the last year, in order, are 75, 75, 77, 76, 77, 78, 80, 80, 81, 82, 83, and 83.
   a. Draw two line graphs of these data, one with a vertical scale of 0 to 100 and the other with a vertical scale of 75 to 83.
   b. What conclusion might you make from the first graph?

   c. What conclusions might you make from the second graph?

3. The incomes of the families in a small mill town are listed in the chart at the right.
   a. Find the mode, median, and mean of the data.

   b. Which number is misleading?
   c. Which would most accurately describe the data?

4. A television commercial says 9 out of 10 doctors recommend Blyer's Aspirin. Do you think this survey is reliable? Why or why not?

Income (to nearest $10,000)	Number of Families
$2,000,000	1
200,000	2
40,000	30
30,000	30
20,000	20
10,000	30
0	40

Mathematics: Applications and Connections, Course 2

4-1

Study Guide

Divisibility Patterns

The following rules will help you determine if a number is divisible by 2, 3, 4, 5, 6, 9, or 10.

A number is divisible by:

- 2 if the digit in the ones place is even.
- 3 if the sum of the digits is divisible by 3.
- 4 if the number formed by the last two digits is divisible by 4.
- 5 if the digit in the ones place is 0 or 5.
- 6 if the number is divisible by 2 and 3.
- 9 if the sum of the digits is divisible by 9.
- 10 if the digit in the ones place is 0.

Example **Determine whether 2,346 is divisible by 2, 3, 4, 5, 6, 9, or 10.**

 2: Yes; the ones digit, 6, is even.

 3: Yes; the sum of the digits, $2 + 3 + 4 + 6 = 15$, is divisible by 3.

 4: No; the number formed by the last two digits, 46, is not divisible by 4.

 5: No; the ones digit is not 0 or 5.

 6: Yes; the number is divisible by 2 and 3.

 9: No; the sum of the digits, 15, is not divisible by 9.

 10: No; the ones digit, 6, is not 0.

 2,346 is divisible by 2, 3, and 6.

Determine whether the first number is divisible by the second number.

1. 65; 5   **2.** 2,641; 3   **3.** 6,780; 10   **4.** 4,185; 9

5. 4,889; 2   **6.** 8,826; 4   **7.** 60,003; 6   **8.** 642; 4

Determine whether each number is divisible by 2, 3, 4, 5, 6, 9, or 10.

9. 660   **10.** 5,025   **11.** 5,091   **12.** 356

Divisibility Patterns

Determine whether the first number is divisible by the second number.

1. 112; 4   **2.** 3,465,870; 5   **3.** 34,456,433; 9

4. 5,653,121; 3   **5.** 6,432; 10   **6.** 3,469; 6

7. 42,981; 2   **8.** 73,125; 3   **9.** 3,522; 6

Determine whether each number is divisible by 2, 3, 4, 5, 6, 9, or 10.

10. 240   **11.** 657   **12.** 8,760

13. 3,408   **14.** 4,605   **15.** 7,800

16. 8,640   **17.** 432   **18.** 8,000

Find two numbers that are divisible by both of the given numbers.

19. 3, 5   **20.** 5, 9   **21.** 6, 10

22. 4, 10   **23.** 9, 6   **24.** 2, 9

4-2 Study Guide

Prime Factorization

A **prime number** is a whole number greater than 1 that has exactly two factors, 1 and itself.

Examples   7   factors: 1, 7

                23   factors: 1, 23

A **composite number** is a whole number greater than 1 that has more than two factors. Every composite number can be written as the product of prime numbers. This is called the **prime factorization** of the number.

Example   **Write the prime factorization of 420.**

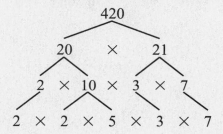

Write 420 as the product of two factors.
Keep factoring until all of the factors are prime numbers.

The prime factorization of 420 is 2 × 2 × 3 × 5 × 7, or $2^2 \times 3 \times 5 \times 7$.

Determine whether each number is composite or prime.

1. 34   **2.** 77   **3.** 37   **4.** 89

5. 69   **6.** 67   **7.** 123   **8.** 71

Write the prime factorization of each number.

9. 490   **10.** 225   **11.** 1,155   **12.** 1,105

Prime Factorization

Determine whether each number is composite or prime.

1. 18

2. 31

3. 434

4. 97

5. 111,111

6. 4,293

Use a factor tree to find the prime factorization of each number.

7. 280

8. 92

9. 900

Use a calculator to find the prime factors of each number. Then write the prime factorization of each number.

10. 66

11. 306

12. 2,475

13. 196

14. 2,400

15. 1,024

16. 225

17. 187

18. 170

Find the missing factor.

19. $3^2 \times 5 \times$ _____ $= 315$

20. $2^4 \times$ _____ $\times 7 = 1,008$

21. $3^3 \times$ _____ $= 135$

22. $2^2 \times 3^2 \times$ _____ $= 252$

23. $5^2 \times$ _____ $= 275$

24. $3^2 \times 5^2 \times$ _____ $= 2,475$

4-3 Study Guide

Integration: Patterns and Functions
Sequences

A **sequence** of numbers is a list in a specific order. The numbers in the sequence are called **terms.**

A sequence is an **arithmetic sequence** if you can always find the next term by adding the same number to the previous term.

Examples   1   7,   11,   15,   19,   23, . . .   *The next term can be found by*
                          +4   +4   +4   +4   *adding 4 to the previous term.*

The next three terms are 27, 31, and 35.

2   76,   73,   70,   67,   64, . . .   *The next term can be found by*
               −3   −3   −3   −3   *subtracting 3 from the previous term.*

The next three terms are 61, 58, and 55.

A sequence is a **geometric sequence** if you can find the next term by multiplying the previous term by the same number.

Example 3   576,   288,   144,   72, . . .   *The next term can be found by*
                 × 0.5   × 0.5   × 0.5   *multiplying the previous term by 0.5.*

The next three terms are 36, 18, and 9.

A sequence may be neither arithmetic nor geometric.

Example 4   3,   4,   6,   9,   13, . . .   *The next term can be found by*
                 +1   +2   +3   +4   *adding one more than the number*
                                                  added to the previous term.

The next three terms are 18, 24, and 31.

Identify each sequence as arithmetic, geometric, or neither.
Then find the next three terms.

1. 89, 86, 83, 80, . . .   **2.** 5, 25, 125, 625, . . .   **3.** 7, 12, 17, 22, . . .

4. 78, 75, 77, 74, 76, . . .   **5.** 64, 32, 16, 8, . . .   **6.** 90, 85, 79, 72, . . .

Integration: Patterns and Functions
Sequences

Describe the pattern in each sequence. Identify the sequence as arithmetic, geometric, or neither. Then find the next three terms.

1. 6, 12, 18, 24, . . .

2. 1, 4, 16, 64, . . .

3. 72, 36, 18, 9, . . .

4. 2, 9, 11, 18, 20, 27, . . .

5. 9, 18, 27, 36, 45, . . .

6. 0.2, 0.4, 0.8, 1.6, . . .

7. 1, 3, 9, 27, . . .

8. 1, 4, 9, 16, 25, . . .

9. 0, 16, 32, 48, 64, . . .

10. 1.2, 2.3, 3.4, 4.5, . . .

11. 1, 5, 25, 125, . . .

12. 210, 211, 213, 216, . . .

Create a sequence using each rule. Provide four terms for the sequence beginning with the given number. State whether the sequence is arithmetic, geometric, or neither.

13. Add 0.4 to each term; 8.

14. Multiply each term by 3; 5.

15. Multiply each term by 0.5; 42.

16. Add 0.3 to the first term, 0.5 to the next term, 0.7 to the next term, and so on; 10.

4-4 Study Guide

Greatest Common Factor

The **greatest common factor (GCF)** of two or more numbers is the greatest number that is a factor of each number. One way to find the GCF is to list the factors of each number and then choose the greatest of the common factors.

Example   **Find the GCF of 72 and 108.**

factors of 72: 1, 2, 3, 4, 6, 8, 9, 12, 18, 24, 36, 72
factors of 108: 1, 2, 3, 4, 6, 9, 12, 18, 27, 36, 54, 108

common factors: 1, 2, 3, 4, 6, 9, 12, 18, 36

The GCF of 72 and 108 is 36.

Another way to find the GCF is to write the prime factorization of each number. Then identify all common prime factors and find their product.

Example   **Find the GCF of 210 and 525.**

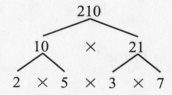   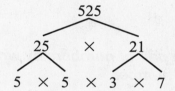

common prime factors: 3, 5, 7

The GCF of 210 and 525 is 3 × 5 × 7 or 105.

Find the GCF of each set of numbers.

1. 18, 30

2. 60, 45

3. 24, 72

4. 32, 48

5. 100, 30

6. 54, 36

7. 120, 200

8. 81, 153

9. 77, 121

10. 60, 24, 72

11. 32, 48, 80

12. 90, 120, 180

Greatest Common Factor

Find the GCF of each set of numbers by listing the factors of each number.

1. 12, 18

2. 16, 30

3. 44, 153

Find the GCF of each pair of numbers by listing the common prime factors of each number.

4. $80 = 2^4 \times 5$
$110 = 2 \times 5 \times 11$

5. $42 = 2 \times 3 \times 7$
$49 = 7 \times 7$

6. $16 = 2^4$
$48 = 2^4 \times 3$

Find the GCF of each pair of numbers by writing the prime factorization of each number.

7. 35, 85

8. 40, 100

9. 42, 23

Find the GCF of each set of numbers.

10. 66, 72

11. 144, 72

12. 9, 11

13. 720, 480

14. 90, 130

15. 12, 33

16. 6, 9, 12

17. 10, 20, 35

18. 64, 80, 120

4-5 Study Guide

Simplifying Fractions and Ratios

A fraction is in **simplest form** when the greatest common factor (GCF) of the numerator and the denominator is 1.

Example 1   Express $\frac{36}{54}$ in simplest form.

factors of 36: 1, 2, 3, 4, 6, 9, 12, 18, 36
factors of 54: 1, 2, 3, 6, 9, 18, 27, 54

The GCF of 36 and 54 is 18.

$\frac{36}{54} = \frac{36 \div 18}{54 \div 18} = \frac{2}{3}$ *Divide the numerator and denominator by the GCF.*

You can also express a ratio in simplest form.

Example 2   Express 28:63 in simplest form.

factors of 28: 1, 2, 4, 7, 14, 28
factors of 63: 1, 3, 7, 9, 21, 63

The GCF of 28 and 63 is 7.

$\frac{28}{63} = \frac{28 \div 7}{63 \div 7} = \frac{4}{9}$ *Divide the numerator and denominator by the GCF.*

Express each fraction or ratio in simplest form.

1. $\frac{30}{72}$

2. 45:60

3. $\frac{68}{84}$

4. 54:66

5. 56:64

6. $\frac{17}{119}$

7. $\frac{60}{75}$

8. $\frac{75}{375}$

9. 36:48

10. 33:132

11. $\frac{450}{750}$

12. 25:125

Mathematics: Applications and Connections, Course 2

Simplifying Fractions and Ratios

Express each fraction or ratio in simplest form.

1. $\frac{25}{35}$

2. 88:55

3. $\frac{32}{160}$

4. $\frac{36}{80}$

5. $\frac{400}{500}$

6. 49:72

7. 140:100

8. 225:625

9. $\frac{232}{144}$

10. $\frac{23}{46}$

11. 750:350

12. $\frac{27}{45}$

13. 80:24

14. $\frac{19}{48}$

15. 180:240

Write two different fractions that can be expressed in simplest form as each of the following.

16. $\frac{1}{4}$

17. $\frac{3}{5}$

18. $\frac{4}{7}$

19. $\frac{1}{7}$

20. $\frac{2}{3}$

21. $\frac{3}{7}$

4-6 Study Guide

Ratios and Percents

A **percent** is a ratio that compares a number to 100.

Examples **1** Write a percent to represent the shaded area of the model.

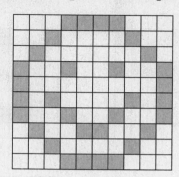

32 out of 100 squares are shaded.
$\frac{32}{100} = 32\%$

2 Express 28:63 as a percent.

$\frac{28}{63} = 44.\overline{4}\%$

Write a percent to represent the shaded area.

1.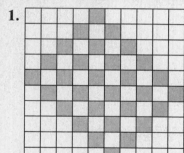

2.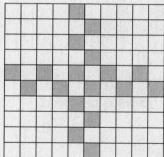

Express each ratio as a percent.

3. $\frac{72}{100}$

4. 45:100

5. 68 people out of 100

6. 66:100

7. 7 to 100

8. 17 in 100

Ratios and Percents

Write a percent to represent the shaded area.

1.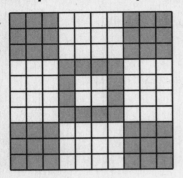

2.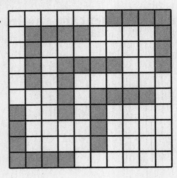

3.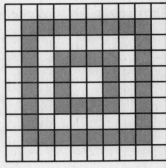

4.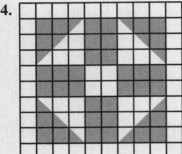

5.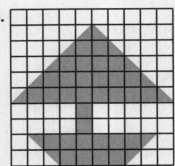

6.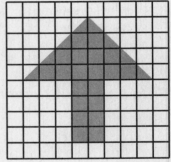

Express each ratio as a percent.

7. $\frac{68}{100}$

8. $\frac{47}{100}$

9. 17 hundredths

10. 19.4 out of 100

11. $16\frac{1}{2}$: 100

12. 74.3 to 100

13. 82 per 100

14. $22 per $100

15. 6 rows out of 100 rows

Mathematics: Applications and Connections, Course 2

4-7 Study Guide

Fractions, Decimals, and Percents

A fraction can be expressed as a percent by finding an equivalent fraction with a denominator of 100.

Example 1   Express $\frac{19}{20}$ as a percent.

$$\overset{\times\,5}{\frac{19}{20}} = \underset{\times\,5}{\frac{95}{100}} = 95\%$$

Since 100 ÷ 20 = 5, multiply the numerator and denominator by 5.

When an equivalent fraction cannot easily be found, express the fraction as a decimal first, and then as a percent.

Example 2   Express $\frac{5}{8}$ as a percent.

5 ÷ 8 = *0.625* or 62.5%

You can also express decimals and percents as fractions.

Examples $0.4 = \frac{4}{10}$ or $\frac{2}{5}$

$$18\% = \frac{18}{100}$$

$$= \frac{18 \div 2}{100 \div 2} \text{ or } \frac{9}{50}$$

Express each fraction as a percent.

1. $\frac{14}{25}$ 2. $\frac{3}{4}$ 3. $\frac{7}{8}$

4. $\frac{7}{10}$ 5. $\frac{6}{50}$ 6. $\frac{13}{20}$

Express each percent or decimal as a fraction in simplest form.

7. 20%   8. 0.60   9. 0.15

10. 72%   11. 54%   12. 0.22

Mathematics: Applications and Connections, Course 2

4-7 Practice

Fractions, Decimals, and Percents

Express each fraction as a percent.

1. $\frac{1}{2}$

2. $\frac{1}{4}$

3. $\frac{2}{5}$

4. $\frac{3}{10}$

5. $\frac{40}{50}$

6. $\frac{7}{7}$

7. $\frac{19}{100}$

8. $\frac{21}{25}$

9. $\frac{3}{20}$

10. $\frac{17}{20}$

11. $\frac{24}{40}$

12. $\frac{24}{25}$

Express each percent or decimal as a fraction in simplest form.

13. 20%

14. 0.48

15. 36%

16. 18%

17. 0.10

18. 0.7

19. 35%

20. 22%

21. 0.64

4-8 | Study Guide

Integration: Probability
Simple Events

If you roll a cube with the numbers 1 through 6 on the faces, there are six possible outcomes: 1, 2, 3, 4, 5, and 6. Each of the outcomes is equally likely to occur. A particular outcome, such as rolling a 5, is an event. Probability is the chance that the event will occur.

$$\text{Probability} = \frac{\text{number of ways an event can occur}}{\text{number of possible outcomes}}$$

Rolling a 5 can occur 1 way out of 6 possible outcomes. So, $P(5) = \frac{1}{6}$.

Example   **Ping-Pong® balls numbered 1 through 25 are placed in a box and one is drawn at random. Find each probability.**

probability of drawing a 12:

$$P(12) = \frac{\text{number of ways 12 can occur}}{\text{number of possible outcomes}} = \frac{1}{25}$$

probability of drawing an odd number:

The odd numbers are 1, 3, 5, 7, 9, 11, 13, 15, 17, 19, 21, 23, and 25. There are thirteen balls with an odd number.

$$P(\text{odd}) = \frac{\text{number of ways an odd number can occur}}{\text{number of possible outcomes}} = \frac{13}{25}$$

The spinner shown is equally likely to stop on each of the regions. Find the probability that the spinner will stop on each of the following.

1. a number less than 5

2. an even number

3. a prime number

4. a multiple of 4

5. a factor of 8

6. 7

A drawer contains 4 blue socks, 8 black socks, and 10 white socks. If one sock is taken out of the drawer without looking, find the probability that each of the following will be drawn. Express each ratio as a fraction in simplest form.

7. a blue sock

8. a black sock

9. a white sock

10. a blue or a black sock

11. a black or a white sock

12. a blue or a white sock

Mathematics: Applications and Connections, Course 2

Practice

Integration: Probability
Simple Events

The spinner shown is equally likely to stop on each of its regions numbered 1 to 16. Find the probability that the spinner will stop on each of the following.

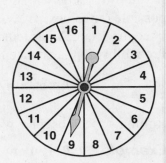

1. an even number

2. a prime number

3. a factor of 10

4. a number less than 7

5. a composite number

6. the GCF of 10 and 15

A bag of marbles contains 3 yellow, 6 blue, 1 green, 12 white, and 8 black marbles. If you reach in the bag and draw one marble at random, what is the probability that you will draw each of the following? Express each ratio as a fraction in simplest form and as a percent.

7. a yellow marble

8. a white marble

9. a blue marble

10. either a black or a green marble

11. a white or a blue marble

A package of candy contains 14 cherry, 16 orange, 10 lemon, and 10 lime flavored candies. If you reach in the package and draw one piece of candy at random, what is the probability that you will select each of the following? Express each ratio as a fraction in simplest form and as a percent.

12. a lemon candy

13. an orange candy

14. a cherry candy

15. an orange or lemon candy

16. a lime, lemon, or cherry candy

17. any candy

18. a candy that is not lemon, lime or cherry

4-9 Study Guide

Least Common Multiple

A **multiple** of a number is the product of that number and any whole number. The least nonzero multiple of two or more numbers is the **least common multiple (LCM)** of the numbers.

Example 1 Find the LCM of 15 and 20.

multiples of 15: 15, 30, 45, 60, 75, 90, 105, 120, . . .
multiples of 20: 20, 40, 60, 80, 100, 120, 140, . . .

The LCM of 15 and 20 is 60.

Prime factorization can also be used to find the LCM.

Example 2 Find the LCM of 8, 12, and 18.

$$8 = 2 \times 2 \times 2$$ *Find the prime factors of each number.*
$$12 = 2 \times 2 \qquad \times 3$$
$$18 = 2 \qquad\qquad \times 3 \times 3$$
$$\quad\ 2 \quad 2 \qquad 3$$ *Find the common factors.*
$$2 \times 2 \times 2 \times 3 \times 3 = 72$$ *Multiply the common factors and any other factors.*

The LCM of 8, 12, and 18 is 72.

Find the LCM of each set of numbers.

1. 12, 16

2. 15, 24

3. 7, 9

4. 8, 10

5. 20, 50

6. 18, 27

7. 30, 21

8. 12, 18

9. 6, 10, 15

10. 3, 7, 10

11. 2, 16, 24

12. 7, 8, 14

Mathematics: Applications and Connections, Course 2

4-9 Practice

Least Common Multiple

Find the LCM of each set of numbers by listing the multiples of each number.

1. 75, 25

2. 40, 50

3. 2, 4, 5

Find the LCM of each set of numbers by writing the prime factorization of each number.

4. 4, 8, 10

5. 11, 8, 22

6. 39, 9, 117

Find the LCM of each set of numbers.

7. 4, 12

8. 15, 12

9. 156, 13

10. 250, 30

11. 3, 4, 13

12. 200, 18

13. 4, 10, 12

14. 48, 16, 3

15. 66, 55, 44

16. 70, 90

17. 29, 58, 4

18. 6, 15, 20

19. 18, 54

20. 30, 65

21. 180, 252

Mathematics: Applications and Connections, Course 2

4-10 Study Guide

Comparing and Ordering Fractions

To compare fractions, rewrite them so they have the same denominator. The **least common denominator (LCD)** of two fractions is the least common multiple of their denominators.

Example 1   Which fraction is greater, $\frac{5}{6}$ or $\frac{3}{4}$?

Find the LCD by listing the multiples of each denominator.

multiples of 6: 6, 12, 18, 24, 30, 36, . . .

multiples of 4: 4, 8, 12, 16, 20, 24, . . .

The LCM of 6 and 4 is 12. So, the LCD of $\frac{5}{6}$ and $\frac{3}{4}$ is 12.

Write $\frac{5}{6}$ and $\frac{3}{4}$ as fractions with a denominator of 12.

$$\overset{\times 2}{\frac{5}{6}} = \frac{10}{12}_{\times 2} \qquad \overset{\times 3}{\frac{3}{4}} = \frac{9}{12}_{\times 3} \qquad \frac{10}{12} > \frac{9}{12}, \text{ so } \frac{5}{6} > \frac{3}{4}.$$

Another way to compare fractions is to express them as decimals. Then compare the decimals.

Example 2   Which fraction is greater, $\frac{7}{9}$ or $\frac{3}{4}$?

Express each fraction as a decimal. Then compare.

$$7 \div 9 = 0.\overline{7} \qquad 3 \div 4 = 0.75 \qquad 0.\overline{7} > 0.75, \text{ so } \frac{7}{9} > \frac{3}{4}.$$

Find the LCD for each pair of fractions.

1. $\frac{1}{2}, \frac{1}{3}$ 2. $\frac{3}{4}, \frac{1}{8}$ 3. $\frac{5}{9}, \frac{1}{2}$ 4. $\frac{2}{3}, \frac{3}{7}$

5. $\frac{5}{9}, \frac{5}{6}$ 6. $\frac{7}{8}, \frac{5}{12}$ 7. $\frac{7}{10}, \frac{4}{5}$ 8. $\frac{3}{4}, \frac{1}{2}$

Replace each $\bigcirc$ with <, > , or = to make a true sentence.

9. $\frac{1}{2} \bigcirc \frac{5}{9}$ 10. $\frac{3}{4} \bigcirc \frac{7}{8}$ 11. $\frac{5}{12} \bigcirc \frac{1}{2}$ 12. $\frac{4}{5} \bigcirc \frac{7}{10}$

4-10 Practice

Comparing and Ordering Fractions

Find the LCD for each pair of fractions.

1. $\frac{4}{7}, \frac{3}{5}$

2. $\frac{5}{12}, \frac{7}{24}$

3. $\frac{6}{28}, \frac{3}{7}$

4. $\frac{7}{15}, \frac{1}{4}$

5. $\frac{7}{11}, \frac{3}{5}$

6. $\frac{5}{17}, \frac{7}{8}$

7. $\frac{5}{12}, \frac{7}{10}$

8. $\frac{15}{16}, \frac{1}{4}$

9. $\frac{5}{8}, \frac{3}{5}$

10. $\frac{5}{16}, \frac{3}{32}$

11. $\frac{7}{13}, \frac{1}{3}$

12. $\frac{7}{9}, \frac{13}{27}$

Replace each ◯ with <, >, or = to make a true sentence.

13. $\frac{3}{4}$ ◯ $\frac{3}{5}$

14. $\frac{5}{8}$ ◯ $\frac{4}{7}$

15. $\frac{4}{9}$ ◯ $\frac{9}{14}$

16. $\frac{7}{11}$ ◯ $\frac{9}{12}$

17. $\frac{6}{10}$ ◯ $\frac{3}{5}$

18. $\frac{7}{12}$ ◯ $\frac{3}{8}$

19. $\frac{3}{5}$ ◯ $\frac{2}{3}$

20. $\frac{21}{30}$ ◯ $\frac{17}{20}$

21. $\frac{8}{13}$ ◯ $\frac{7}{19}$

22. $\frac{1}{6}$ ◯ $\frac{1}{7}$

23. $\frac{2}{3}$ ◯ $\frac{3}{2}$

24. $\frac{8}{24}$ ◯ $\frac{4}{12}$

Mathematics: Applications and Connections, Course 2

5-1 Study Guide

Integers

Integers greater than 0 are **positive integers.** Integers less than 0 are **negative integers.**

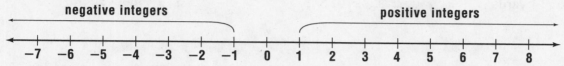

Two numbers are **opposites** if, on the number line, they are the same distance from 0, but on opposite sides of 0. The number line below shows that −5 and 5 are opposites.

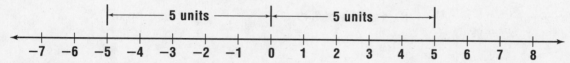

The **absolute value** of an integer is its distance from 0 on the number line.

5 is 5 units from 0.   The absolute value of 5 is 5. $|5| = 5$
−5 is 5 units from 0.   The absolute value of −5 is 5. $|-5| = 5$

Write an integer for each situation.

1. 6°F below zero

2. a gain of 40 pounds

3. a profit of $4

4. a loss of 10 points

5. 68°F above zero

6. falling 3 feet

Write the integer represented by the point for each letter. Then find its opposite and its absolute value.

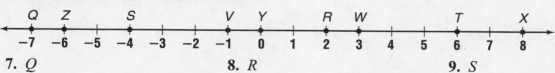

7. Q

8. R

9. S

10. T

11. V

12. W

13. X

14. Y

15. Z

Mathematics: Applications and Connections, Course 2

5-1 Practice

Integers

Write an integer for each situation.

1. a gain of 14 yards

2. a loss of $15

3. 24° above zero

4. 3 points lost

5. a deposit of $40

6. a withdrawal of $100

7. 9° below zero

8. a profit of $49

9. a drop of 18°

10. a loss of 10 pounds

11. a bonus of $140

12. a wage increase of $150

Write the integer represented by the point for each letter. Then find its opposite and its absolute value.

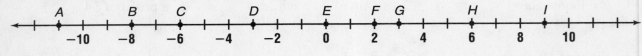

13. A

14. B

15. C

16. D

17. E

18. F

19. G

20. H

21. I

22. What is the least positive integer?

23. A submarine is 2,000 meters below sea level. Write this depth as an integer.

5-2 Study Guide

Comparing and Ordering Integers

To compare or order integers, think of a number line. The number farther to the right on the number line is greater.

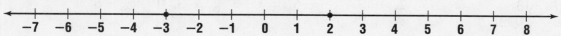

Since 2 is to the right of -3 on the number line, $-3 < 2$.

Examples **1** **Replace each $\bigcirc$ with < or > to make a true sentence.**

$-3 \bigcirc 3$ Since a negative integer is always less than a positive integer, $-3 < 3$.

$-2 \bigcirc -5$ Since -2 is to the right of the -5 on the number line, $-2 > -5$.

2 **Order the integers 0, 3, -1, -3, and 5 from least to greatest.**

-3 is farthest to the left on the number line, so it is least.

Order the integers from left to right.
$-3, -1, 0, 3, 5$

Replace each $\bigcirc$ with < or > to make a true sentence.

1. $-5 \bigcirc 7$
2. $0 \bigcirc -2$
3. $-8 \bigcirc 8$
4. $1 \bigcirc -4$
5. $17 \bigcirc 25$
6. $-12 \bigcirc -10$

Order the integers from least to greatest.

7. $12, -4, 31, 0, -50, -12$

8. $9, -7, 1, -5, 23, -11$

9. $-45, 62, -64, 45, -12, 17$

10. $-2, -14, -8, -19, -24, -1$

11. $-6, 5, 1, -8, 0, -7$

12. $-101, -102, -103, 101, 102, 103$

Mathematics: Applications and Connections, Course 2

5-2 Practice

Comparing and Ordering Integers

Replace each ◯ *with < or > to make a true sentence.*

1. -6 ◯ -13

2. -13 ◯ -6

3. 0 ◯ -8

4. -18 ◯ -98

5. -32 ◯ -23

6. -462 ◯ -46

7. -1 ◯ 1

8. 12 ◯ -12

9. -4 ◯ -6

10. -9 ◯ 0

11. 7 ◯ -3

12. 9 ◯ -99

13. -2 ◯ -22

14. 0 ◯ 8

15. -8 ◯ 8

Order the integers from least to greatest.

16. $3, -5, 8, -10, -18, 24$

17. $-9, -4, 19, 32, -34, -18, -2$

18. $-92, 76, 54, -89, 8, 24, 0$

19. $-54, -76, 9, -7, -45, 65, 43, 2$

20. $-12, -34, 8, -1, 5, -6, 54$

21. $-43, -9, 0, 6, -2, -6, 14, 7$

Mathematics: Applications and Connections, Course 2

5-3 Study Guide

Integration: Geometry
The Coordinate System

The **coordinate system** is used to graph points in a plane. The horizontal line is the **x-axis.** The vertical line is the **y-axis.** Their intersection is the **origin.**

Points are located using **ordered pairs.** The first number in an ordered pair is the **x-coordinate;** the second number is the **y-coordinate.**

Examples

1 **Name the ordered pair for point P.**
Start at the origin.
Move 4 units left along the x-axis.
Move 3 units up on the y-axis.
The ordered pair for point P is $(-4, 3)$.

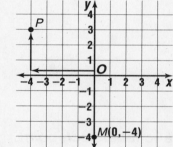

2 **Graph the point $M(0, -4)$.**
Start at the origin.
Move 0 units along the x-axis.
Move 4 units down on the y-axis.
Draw a point and label it M.

Name the x-coordinate and the y-coordinate for each point labeled at the right.

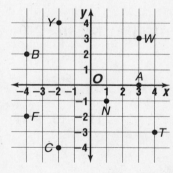

1. B

2. T

3. W

4. C

5. F

6. N

7. A

8. Y

Graph and label each point on the coordinate plane.

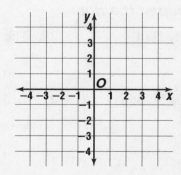

9. $H(-2, 1)$

10. $Q(0, 4)$

11. $D(4, 2)$

12. $E(4, -4)$

13. $G(-4, -4)$

14. $J(0, 0)$

15. $K(-4, 3)$

16. $M(-3, -2)$

5-3 Practice

Integration: Geometry
The Coordinate System

Name the x-coordinate and the y-coordinate for each point labeled at the right. Then tell in which quadrant each point lies.

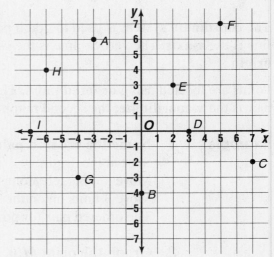

1. *A*   2. *B*   3. *C*

4. *D*   5. *E*   6. *F*

7. *G*   8. *H*   9. *I*

Graph and label each point.

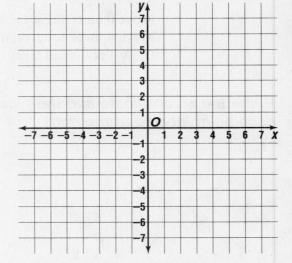

10. $N(-1, 3)$ 11. $V(2, -4)$ 12. $C(6, 0)$

13. $P(-4, 4)$ 14. $M(-2, 0)$ 15. $K(-1, 5)$

16. $T(-3, -3)$ 17. $A(5, -1)$ 18. $D(0, -5)$

Name the ordered pair for each point on the city map at the right.

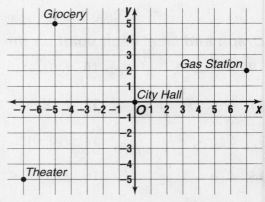

19. City Hall   20. Theater

21. Gas Station   22. Grocery

Mathematics: Applications and Connections, Course 2

5-4 Study Guide

Adding Integers

To add integers, think of a number line. Locate the first addend on the number line. Move right if the second addend is positive. Move left if the second addend is negative.

Example 1 Solve $t = 4 + (-10)$.

Start at 0. Since 4 is positive, go 4 units to the right.
Since -10 is negative, go 10 units to the left.

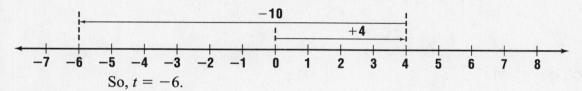

So, $t = -6$.

When you add integers, remember the following.
The sum of two positive integers is positive.
The sum of two negative integers is negative.
The sum of a positive integer and a negative integer is:
- positive if the positive integer has the greater absolute value.
- negative if the negative integer has the greater absolute value.

Examples **2** Solve $n = 14 + (-11)$.

$|14| > |-11|$,
so the sum is positive.
$14 - 11 = 3$
So, $n = 3$.

3 Solve $-24 + 16 = k$.

$|-24| > |16|$,
so the sum is negative.
$24 - 16 = 8$
So, $k = -8$.

Solve each equation.

1. $p = 16 + (-11)$

2. $-22 + (-7) = g$

3. $y = -6 + 36$

4. $-50 + 50 = v$

5. $c = -10 + (-10)$

6. $k = 12 + 9$

7. $100 + (-25) = w$

8. $n = 38 + (-6)$

9. $-50 + (-20) = v$

10. $r = -89 + 29$

11. $85 + (-10) = t$

12. $4 + (-10) = z$

Evaluate each expression if $a = 8$, $b = -8$, and $c = 4$.

13. $a + 16$

14. $b + (-9)$

15. $b + c$

16. $-10 + c$

17. $a + (-21)$

18. $12 + b$

5-4 Practice

Adding Integers

Tell whether the sum is positive, negative, or 0.

1. $5 + (-5)$

2. $-8 + (-3)$

3. $-4 + 7$

4. $9 + (-3)$

5. $-6 + 12$

6. $-5 + (-9)$

Solve each equation.

7. $d = 5 + (-8)$

8. $-6 + 6 = t$

9. $v = -4 + (-9)$

10. $-7 + 13 = h$

11. $n = 9 + (-9)$

12. $b = 14 + (-27)$

13. $y = 15 + (-10)$

14. $19 + (-10) = k$

15. $-12 + (-18) = s$

16. $-14 + (-12) = p$

17. $m = -12 + (-8)$

18. $c = -28 + 16$

Evaluate each expression if $a = -8$, $b = 12$, and $c = -4$.

19. $a + (-6)$

20. $-10 + b$

21. $c + (-7)$

22. $a + b$

23. $c + 0$

24. $b + c$

5-5 Study Guide

Subtracting Integers

An integer and its **opposite** are the same distance from 0 on a number line.
The integers 5 and −5 are opposites.

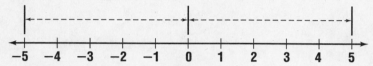

The sum of an integer and its opposite is 0.
$$-5 + 5 = 0$$

To subtract an integer, add its opposite.

Examples   **1**   Solve $t = 6 - 9$.
$t = 6 + (-9)$ *To subtract 9, add −9.*
$t = -3$

2   Solve $m = -10 - (-12)$.
$m = -10 + 12$ *To subtract −12, add 12.*
$m = 2$

Solve each equation.

1. $b = 8 - 11$

2. $18 - (-5) = p$

3. $-10 - 4 = h$

4. $n = -8 - (-6)$

5. $v = -15 - 40$

6. $x = 25 - (-13)$

7. $51 - (-26) = k$

8. $-30 - (-52) = a$

9. $95 - 101 = m$

10. $j = -75 - 50$

11. $r = 5 - 55$

12. $19 - (-10) = y$

Evaluate each expression if $m = -1$, $n = 10$, and $p = 6$.

13. $m - 8$

14. $10 - m$

15. $-n - p$

16. $n - m$

17. $p - (-m)$

18. $-25 - p$

*Mathematics: Applications
and Connections, Course 2*

5-5 Practice

Subtracting Integers

Solve each equation.

1. $j = 6 - (-8)$

2. $-2 - 3 = t$

3. $y = -8 - (-10)$

4. $9 - 14 = k$

5. $s = 36 - (-12)$

6. $5 - 12 = f$

7. $n = 15 - (-8)$

8. $-16 - 6 = v$

9. $m = -4 - 9$

10. $-17 - 13 = h$

11. $g = 12 - (-9)$

12. $b = 14 - (-22)$

13. $x = 5 - (-25)$

14. $-19 - (-50) = a$

15. $12 - (-52) = w$

Evaluate each expression if r = −6, s = 10, and t = −8.

16. $r - 8$

17. $t - s$

18. $-12 - r$

19. $t - r$

20. $s - t$

21. $r - s$

5-6 Study Guide

Multiplying Integers

The product of two positive integers is positive.

Examples Solve $m = 5(8)$.
$m = 40$

Solve $n = 4(5)(6)$.
$n = 20(6)$
$n = 120$

Solve $p = (2)(8)(1)$.
$p = 16(1)$
$p = 16$

The product of two negative integers is positive.

Examples Solve $y = (-6)(-9)$.
$y = 54$

Solve $x = (-7)^2$.
$x = (-7)(-7)$
$x = 49$

Solve $z = (-3)(-5)(2)$.
$z = 15(2)$
$z = 30$

The product of a positive integer and a negative integer is negative.

Examples Solve $d = (-4)(7)$.
$d = -28$

Solve $e = (10)(-5)(3)$.
$e = -50(3)$
$e = -150$

Solve $f = (-9)(2)^2$.
$f = (-9)(4)$
$f = -36$

Solve each equation.

1. $-7(-8) = p$

2. $10(-6) = j$

3. $a = -9(3)$

4. $(-8)^2 = k$

5. $m = (-12)(-12)$

6. $20(-20) = v$

7. $t = (-25)(4)$

8. $15(30) = c$

9. $h = 2(-2)(2)$

Evaluate each expression if $x = -3$, $y = -10$, $a = 2$, and $b = 6$.

10. $-8a$

11. $9x$

12. xy

13. ab

14. $3xa$

15. $-10by$

16. $-abx$

17. x^2

18. $25y$

5-6 Practice

Multiplying Integers

Solve each equation.

1. $m = 2(-8)$

2. $-3(-4) = t$

3. $x = 8(-4)$

4. $(-5)(-5) = p$

5. $r = -12(5)$

6. $(-4)^2 = w$

7. $e = -12(13)$

8. $14(-3) = v$

9. $n = -14(-5)$

10. $(-11)^2 = h$

11. $d = -7(-8)$

12. $b = -9(10)$

Evaluate each expression if $m = -6$, $n = 3$, and $p = -4$.

13. $-4m$

14. np

15. $2mn$

16. $-2m^2$

17. $-5np$

18. $-10mp$

19. $-12np$

20. mnp

21. p^2

Mathematics: Applications and Connections, Course 2

5-7 Study Guide

Dividing Integers

If two integers have the same sign, their quotient is positive.

Examples

1 Solve $k = 560 \div 8$. *The signs are the same.*
$k = 70$ *The quotient is positive.*

2 Solve $h = -120 \div (-6)$. *The signs are the same.*
$h = 20$ *The quotient is positive.*

If two integers have different signs, their quotient is negative.

Examples

3 Solve $a = -75 \div 5$. *The dividend is negative.*
$a = -15$ *The divisor is positive.*
The quotient is negative.

4 Solve $b = 99 \div (-33)$. *The dividend is positive.*
$b = -3$ *The divisor is negative.*
The quotient is negative.

Solve each equation.

1. $y = 64 \div (-8)$

2. $-100 \div 4 = c$

3. $f = -250 \div (-5)$

4. $60 \div (-12) = x$

5. $-90 \div (-10) = u$

6. $-88 \div 4 = k$

7. $375 \div (-25) = g$

8. $t = -960 \div (-3)$

9. $r = 700 \div 35$

Evaluate each expression if $r = -96$, $t = -8$, and $v = 2$.

10. $\frac{r}{t}$

11. $\frac{t}{v}$

12. $\frac{-4r}{t}$

13. $\frac{t^2}{v}$

14. $\frac{728}{t}$

15. $\frac{tv}{4}$

16. $\frac{r}{-48}$

17. $\frac{4t}{v}$

18. $\frac{r}{tv}$

5-7 Practice

Dividing Integers

Solve each equation.

1. $f = -16 \div (-4)$

2. $-100 \div 10 = v$

3. $m = -28 \div 7$

4. $52 \div (-4) = g$

5. $d = -125 \div (-25)$

6. $-32 \div (-16) = q$

7. $e = -120 \div (-12)$

8. $45 \div (-9) = r$

9. $p = 33 \div (-3)$

10. $-36 \div 12 = z$

11. $d = -200 \div (-25)$

12. $c = -88 \div 11$

Evaluate each expression if $e = -36$, $f = 4$, and $g = -3$.

13. $\frac{e}{f}$

14. $-48 \div g$

15. $\frac{e}{fg}$

16. $e^2 \div f$

17. $\frac{e}{g^2}$

18. $eg \div f$

19. $\frac{e^2}{fg}$

20. $\frac{-100}{f}$

21. $\frac{e^2}{g^2}$

5-8 Study Guide

Integration: Geometry
Graphing Transformations

One kind of transformation is a **reflection**. A reflection is a flip.
Multiply the x-coordinate by -1 to reflect over the y-axis.
Multiply the y-coordinate by -1 to reflect over the x-axis.

Example 1 $\triangle ABC$ has vertices $A(1, 2)$, $B(4, 3)$ and
$C(3, -1)$. **Graph its reflection over the**
y-axis.

Multiply each x-coordinate by -1.
$A(1, 2) \rightarrow A'(-1, 2)$
$B(4, 3) \rightarrow B'(-4, 3)$
$C(3, -1) \rightarrow C'(-3, -1)$

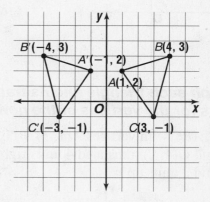

Another type of transformation is a **translation**. A
translation is a slide.

Example 2 $\triangle LMN$ has vertices $L(2, -2)$,
$M(-1, -3)$ and $N(-1, 1)$. **Translate**
$\triangle LMN$ **2 units up and 3 units right.**

Add 3 to each x-coordinate. Add 2 to
each y-coordinate.

$L(2, -2) \rightarrow (2 + 3, -2 + 2) \rightarrow L'(5, 0)$
$M(-1, -3) \rightarrow (-1 + 3, -3 + 2) \rightarrow M'(2, -1)$
$N(-1, 1) \rightarrow (-1 + 3, 1 + 2) \rightarrow N'(2, 3)$

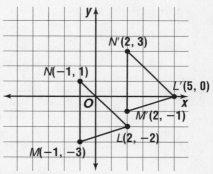

Graph each triangle and its transformation. Write the ordered
pairs for the vertices of the new triangle.

1. $\triangle DEF$ with vertices $D(1, 2)$, $E(5, 3)$
   and $F(5, 0)$ reflected over the y-axis

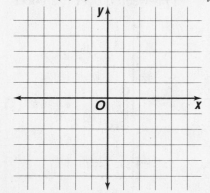

2. $\triangle QRS$ with vertices $Q(-6, -2)$,
   $R(-1, 0)$ and $S(-1, 3)$ translated 1 unit
   up and 7 units right

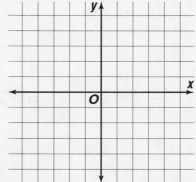

*Mathematics: Applications
and Connections*, Course 2

5-8 Practice

Integration: Geometry
Graphing Transformations

Classify each graph as a reflection or translation.

1.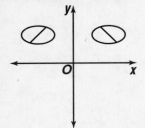

2.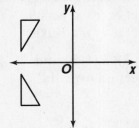

3.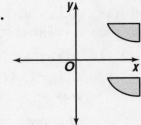

Graph each triangle and its transformation. Write the ordered pairs for the vertices of the new figure.

4. $\triangle ABC$ with vertices $A(1, 3)$, $B(1, 1)$, and $C(4, 1)$ translated 4 units right and 2 units up

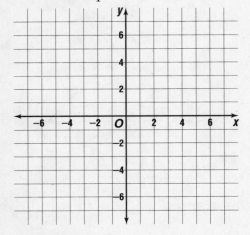

5. $\triangle DEF$ with vertices $D(-1, 4)$, $E(1, -1)$, and $F(-2, 2)$ translated 4 units left and 3 units down

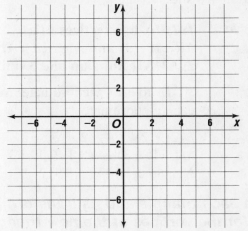

6. $\triangle GHI$ with vertices $G(-1, 3)$, $H(-4, 2)$, and $I(-2, 4)$ reflected over the x-axis

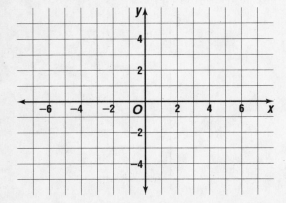

7. $\triangle JKL$ with vertices $J(5, 1)$, $K(-1, 4)$, and $L(-3, -1)$ reflected over the y-axis

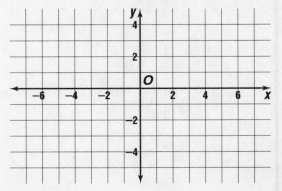

6-1 Study Guide

Solving Addition and Subtraction Equations

Remember, equations must always remain balanced. If you add the same number to each side of an equation, the two sides remain equal.

Example 1 Solve $t - 12.2 = 15.3$. Check your solution.

$$t - 12.2 + 12.2 = 15.3 + 12.2 \qquad \textit{Add 12.2 to each side of the equation.}$$
$$t = 27.5$$

Check: $t - 12.2 = 15.3$
   $27.5 - 12.2 \stackrel{?}{=} 15.3 \qquad \textit{Replace t with 27.5.}$
   $15.3 = 15.3$ ✔

If you subtract the same number from each side of an equation, the two sides remain equal.

Example 2 Solve $5\frac{2}{5} + v = 7\frac{1}{2}$. Check your solution.

$$5\frac{2}{5} - 5\frac{2}{5} + v = 7\frac{1}{2} - 5\frac{2}{5} \qquad \textit{Subtract } 5\frac{2}{5} \textit{ from each side of the equation.}$$
$$v = 7\frac{5}{10} - 5\frac{4}{10}$$
$$v = 2\frac{1}{10}$$

Check: $5\frac{2}{5} + v = 7\frac{1}{2}$
   $5\frac{2}{5} + 2\frac{1}{10} \stackrel{?}{=} 7\frac{1}{2} \qquad \textit{Replace v with } 2\frac{1}{10}.$
   $5\frac{4}{10} + 2\frac{1}{10} \stackrel{?}{=} 7\frac{1}{2}$
   $7\frac{5}{10} \stackrel{?}{=} 7\frac{1}{2}$
   $7\frac{1}{2} = 7\frac{1}{2}$ ✔

Solve each equation. Check your solution.

1. $17 + k = 62$

2. $j - 4.5 = 1.7$

3. $8.9 = p - 3.3$

4. $n + 2\frac{1}{3} = 4\frac{2}{3}$

5. $17.2 = h + 4.9$

6. $y - 9 = 29$

7. $133 = v + 70$

8. $x - 7\frac{1}{2} = 15$

9. $146 + j = 199$

10. $m - 9.4 = 15.7$

11. $89.6 = c + 62.2$

12. $f - 19 = 77$

6-1 **Practice**

Solving Addition and Subtraction Equations

Solve each equation. Check your solution.

1. $y + 18 = 39$

2. $m - 23 = 17$

3. $74 = d + 37$

4. $w + 6 = 19$

5. $n - 4.7 = 8.4$

6. $s - 5 = 12$

7. $m + 18 = 78$

8. $12\frac{3}{4} + y = 32\frac{1}{8}$

9. $18.42 + t = 63$

10. $p - 12 = 34$

11. $b - 43 = 18$

12. $48 = t - 63$

13. $d + 2.6 = 7.1$

14. $h - 32\frac{3}{5} = 44$

15. $e - 0.9 = 17.4$

16. $26 = y - 87$

17. $13.2 + f = 17.4$

18. $25\frac{2}{3} = k - 2\frac{1}{6}$

19. $104 = a - 14$

20. $a + 34 = 90$

21. $e + 12.2 = 40$

6-2 Study Guide

Solving Multiplication Equations

If you divide each side of an equation by the same nonzero number, the two sides remain equal.

Example 1 Solve $48.6 = 6c$. **Check your solution.**

$$\frac{48.6}{6} = \frac{6c}{6} \qquad\qquad \textit{Divide each side of the equation by 6.}$$
$$8.1 = c$$

Check: $48.6 = 6c$
$48.6 \stackrel{?}{=} 6 \times 8.1 \qquad \textit{Replace c with 8.1.}$
$48.6 = 48.6$ ✔

If you multiply each side of an equation by the same number, the two sides remain equal.

Example 2 Solve $\frac{w}{5} = 2.3$. **Check your solution.**

$$\frac{w}{5} \cdot 5 = 2.3 \times 5 \qquad \textit{Multiply each side of the equation by 5.}$$
$$w = 11.5$$

Check: $\frac{w}{5} = 2.3$
$\frac{11.5}{5} \stackrel{?}{=} 2.3 \qquad \textit{Replace w with 11.5.}$
$2.3 = 2.3$ ✔

Solve each equation. Check your solution.

1. $5r = 45$

2. $\frac{y}{7} = 3.5$

3. $180 = 9v$

4. $21 = \frac{n}{3}$

5. $\frac{1}{5}x = 4$

6. $\frac{f}{1.1} = 7$

7. $\frac{1}{2} = \frac{1}{8} \cdot c$

8. $17v = 289$

9. $3.5 = \frac{m}{4}$

10. $\frac{y}{5} = 2.4$

11. $5.1p = 61.2$

12. $0.6 = \frac{a}{9}$

13. $\frac{x}{10} = 4.9$

14. $6.4t = 64$

15. $\frac{s}{8} = 9.6$

Mathematics: Applications and Connections, Course 2

6-2 **Practice**

Solving Multiplication Equations

Solve each equation. Check your solution.

1. $12h = 48$

2. $\frac{m}{8} = 7$

3. $34 = \frac{r}{3}$

4. $4n = 52$

5. $\frac{y}{12} = 18$

6. $49 = \frac{t}{5}$

7. $64 = 2v$

8. $23 = \frac{b}{7}$

9. $\frac{x}{2} = 20$

10. $1.8a = 0.9$

11. $\frac{b}{3.5} = 7.3$

12. $195 = 15s$

13. $\frac{p}{2.8} = 0.6$

14. $121 = 11d$

15. $1.5z = 7.5$

16. $c \div \frac{1}{4} = \frac{1}{2}$

17. $4.8g = 15.36$

18. $h \div 12 = 4.8$

Mathematics: Applications and Connections, Course 2

6-3

Study Guide

Solving Two-Step Equations

To solve two-step equations, you need to add or subtract first.
You also need to multiply or divide.

Examples **1** Solve $7v - 3 = 25$.

$$7v - 3 = 25$$
$$7v - 3 + 3 = 25 + 3 \qquad \text{Add 3 to each side of the equation.}$$
$$7v = 28$$
$$\frac{7v}{7} = \frac{28}{7} \qquad \text{Divide each side of the equation by 7.}$$
$$v = 4$$

2 Solve $\frac{1}{6}(r - 3) = -5$.

$$\frac{1}{6}(r - 3) = -5$$
$$6 \times \frac{1}{6}(r - 3) = 6(-5) \qquad \text{Multiply each side by 6.}$$
$$r - 3 = -30$$
$$r - 3 + 3 = -30 + 3 \qquad \text{Add 3 to each side of the equation.}$$
$$r = -27$$

Solve each equation. Check your solution.

1. $\frac{1}{3}(s + 6) = 3$

2. $\frac{1}{5}(t - 2) = 0$

3. $\frac{2}{3}(a - 18) = -6$

4. $12 - 4n = 4$

5. $7 + \frac{k}{4} = 9$

6. $\frac{1}{2}y - 7 = -9$

7. $\frac{2}{3}(b + 6) = -2$

8. $\frac{3}{8}(c + 8) = -\frac{3}{2}$

9. $\frac{5}{7}(d + 20) = -10$

10. $14 + \frac{t}{5} = 10$

11. $\frac{-h}{6} + 1 = -1$

12. $-5t - 5 = -5$

6-3 Practice

Solving Two-Step Equations

Solve each equation. Check your solution.

1. $6n - 2 = 22$

2. $0.5(y - 3) = 12$

3. $4x - 5 = 15$

4. $\frac{w}{-3} + 14 = 5$

5. $1.5s - 8 = 19$

6. $24 = 17 - 2c$

7. $6 - 3b = -9$

8. $-5h - 6 = 24$

9. $\frac{n}{3} - 6 = 12$

10. $3n + 12 = -12$

11. $7x + 2 = 23$

12. $9 = 16d + 51$

13. $3 = -3y - 15$

14. $174 = 75 + 55t$

15. $2n + 35 = 106$

16. $1.2x + 3.7 = 34.6$

17. $3q + 7 = 13$

18. $-12 = 7s - 5$

19. $7t - 3 = 10$

20. $9y + 4 = 4$

21. $8w + 2 = -2$

6-4 Study Guide

Writing Expressions and Equations

The table below shows phrases written as mathematical expressions.

Phrases	Expression	Phrases	Expression
9 more than a number the sum of 9 and a number a number plus 9 a number increased by 9 the total of x and 9	$x + 9$	4 subtracted from a number a number minus 4 4 less than a number a number decreased by 4 the difference of h and 4	$h - 4$
Phrases	**Expression**	**Phrases**	**Expression**
6 multiplied by g 6 times a number the product of g and 6	$6g$	a number divided by 5 the quotient of t and 5 divide a number by 5	$\dfrac{t}{5}$

The table below shows sentences written as an equation.

Sentences	Equation
Sixty less than three times the amount is $59. Three times the amount less 60 is equal to 59. 59 is equal to 60 subtracted from three times a number. A number times three minus 60 equals 59.	$3n - 60 = 59$

Write each phrase as an algebraic expression.

1. 7 less than m

2. the quotient of 3 and y

3. the total of 5 and c

4. the difference of 6 and r

5. n divided by 2

6. the product of k and 9

Write each sentence as an algebraic equation.

7. A number increased by 7 is 11.

8. The price decreased by $4 is $29.

9. Twice as many points as Bob would be 18 points.

10. After dividing the money 5 ways, each person got $67.

11. Three more than 8 times as many trees is 75 trees.

12. Seven less than a number is 15.

6-4 Practice

Writing Expressions and Equations

Write each phrase as an algebraic expression.

1. thirteen plus *v*

2. three times *d*

3. six less *w*

4. the product of 5 and a number

5. *g* divided by 6

6. the difference of *h* and 8

7. three more hits than Bob

8. 23 divided into *y*

9. twice Michael's age

10. $18 less than the sale price

11. three higher than Kyra's score

12. the quotient of *n* and 12

Write each sentence as an algebraic equation.

13. Juan's salary plus $125 is $600.

14. Fourteen divided by a number is 21.

15. Four times the number of feet is 12 feet.

16. Six times as many visitors is 120 visitors.

17. Twenty-seven is seven fewer students than last year.

18. The number of cats decreased by 17 is 19.

19. Two and one-half times the amount of interest is $2,500.

20. One hundred increased by a number is 537.

6-5 Study Guide

Inequalities

An inequality is a mathematical sentence that contains the symbols $<$, $>$, $\leq$, or $\geq$.

Words	Symbols
m is greater than 7.	$m > 7$
r is less than -4.	$r < -4$
t is greater than or equal to 6.	$t \geq 6$
y is less than or equal to 1.	$y \leq 1$

Solve inequalities just like you solve equations.
You can use a number line to show solutions to inequalities.

Examples

1 Solve $v + 3 < 5$.
Then graph the solution.

$$v + 3 < 5$$
$$v + 3 - 3 < 5 - 3$$
$$v < 2$$

This point is not included.

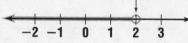

2 Solve $\frac{k}{4} \geq 2$.
Then graph the solution.

$$\frac{k}{4} > 2$$
$$\frac{k}{4} \times 4 \geq 2 \times 4$$
$$k \geq 8$$

This point is included.

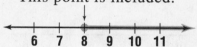

Solve each inequality. Graph the solution on the number line.

1. $c - 1 < 4$

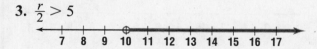

2. $4 + t > -1$

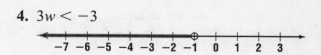

3. $\frac{r}{2} > 5$

4. $3w < -3$

5. $2p \geq 6$

6. $v - 4 \leq 3$

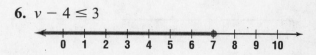

6-5 Practice

Inequalities

Solve each inequality. Graph the solution on a number line.

1. $m + 6 > 10$

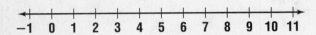

2. $p - 8 < -2$

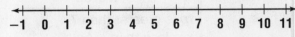

3. $9s \geq 27$

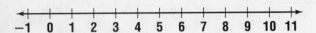

4. $\frac{k}{2} < -3$

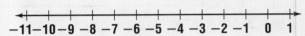

5. $4 + r > -5$

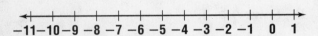

6. $8b \leq 40$

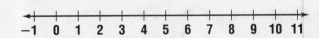

7. $x - 9 \geq -16$

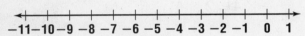

8. $\frac{h}{3} \leq 3$

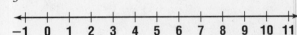

9. $f + 2 \geq -6$

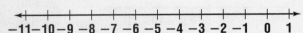

10. $n - 5 < -7$

11. $4t \geq -16$

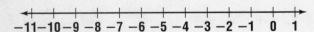

12. $\frac{c}{5} > -2$

13. $6y + 3 \leq -15$

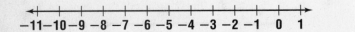

14. $7j - 9 < 47$

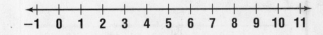

15. $2d - 8 > -18$

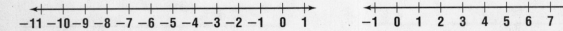

16. $\frac{1}{2}k - 1 \leq 4$

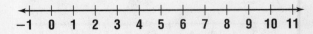

Mathematics: Applications and Connections, Course 2

6-6 Study Guide

Functions and Graphs

The table at the right shows the risk of high blood pressure for people in seven different age groups.
a. Graph the ordered pairs (age, percentage).
b. Describe how the risk of high blood pressure is related to age.
c. When is the increase the greatest?

Age	Americans with High Blood Pressure
18-29	4%
30-39	11%
40-49	21%
50-59	44%
60-69	54%
70-79	64%
80+	65%

Source: *Archives of Internal Medicine,* 1993

a.

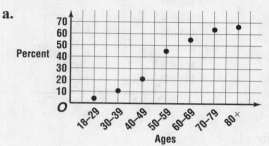

b. The risk of high blood pressure increases as you age.

c. The risk increases greatly once a person reaches the 50-59 age bracket.

Solve.

1. The table below shows the number of adult memberships at sport clubs.

a. Graph the ordered pairs (year, memberships) on the coordinate plane.
b. Write a statement that describes the trend in memberships.

Year	Memberships (in millions)
1987	14
1989	16
1991	16
1993	18
1995	19

Source: International Health, Racquet, and Sportsclub Association

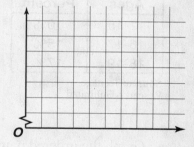

2. The table below shows the average monthly household cable bill for 1990-1996.

a. Graph the ordered pairs (year, bill) on the coordinate plane.
b. Describe the trend of cable bills over time.

Year	Average Cable Bill
1990	$17.60
1991	$19.20
1992	$20.62
1993	$22.49
1994	$21.60
1995	$23.07
1996	$25.50

Source: *USA TODAY*

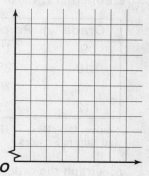

6-6 Practice

Functions and Graphs

Solve.

1. The table below shows the cost of raising a child from birth to age 18.

Year	Cost
1963	$26,000
1973	$38,000
1983	$84,000
1993	$133,000

Source: *Good Housekeeping,*
May, 1995

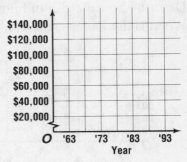

a. Graph the ordered pairs (year, cost) on the coordinate plane.
b. Write a statement that describes the trend over time.

2. The table below shows the percent of teens ages 12-19 who owned pagers or beepers in 1996.

Ages	Percent
12-15	10%
16-17	15%
18-19	17%

Source: Teenage
Research Unlimited

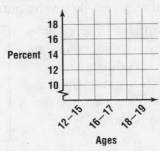

a. Graph the ordered pairs (age, percent) on the coordinate plane.
b. Write a statement that desctibes this relationship as a function.

3. The table below shows the percent of students in grades 9-12 who are enrolled in P. E., or physical education, classes.

Grade	Percent
9	81%
10	72%
11	47%
12	42%

Source: U. S. Dept. of Health
and Human Services

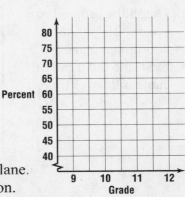

a. Graph the ordered pairs (grade, percent) on the coordinate plane.
b. Write a statement that describes this relationship as a function.

*Mathematics: Applications
and Connections,* Course 2

6-7 Study Guide

Functions and Equations

If the graph of the solutions for an equation is a straight line, the equation is a linear equation.

Example   **Graph $y = \frac{1}{2}x + 1$.**

Select any four values for x. We chose -2, 0, 2, and 4. Substitute these values for x to find y and complete the table of values.

x	$\frac{1}{2}x + 1$	y	(x, y)
-2	$\frac{1}{2}(-2) + 1$	0	$(-2, 0)$
0	$\frac{1}{2}(0) + 1$	1	$(0, 1)$
2	$\frac{1}{2}(2) + 1$	2	$(2, 2)$
4	$\frac{1}{2}(4) + 1$	3	$(4, 3)$

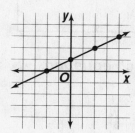

Graph the ordered pairs. Draw a line through all the points.

Graph each equation.

1. $y = 2x$

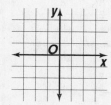

2. $y = x + 2$

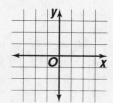

3. $y = -\frac{1}{2}x$

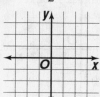

4. $y = -x + 1$

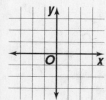

5. $y = x - 1$

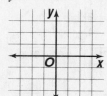

6. $y = -x$

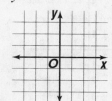

Mathematics: Applications and Connections, Course 2

6-7 Practice

Functions and Equations

Complete each table.

1. $y = 4x$

x	y	(x, y)
2		
1		
0		
−1		

2. $y = 2x - 1$

x	y	(x, y)
−1		
0		
1		
2		

3. $y = -\frac{1}{3}x$

x	y	(x, y)
−3		
0		
3		
6		

Graph each equation.

4. $y = 3x$

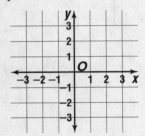

5. $y = x - 4$

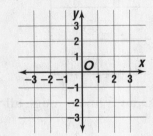

6. $y = -x + 3$

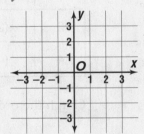

7. $y = -2x + 1$

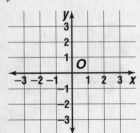

8. $y = 3x + 1$

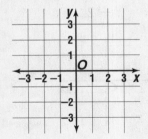

9. $y = -\frac{1}{2}x - 2$

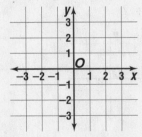

10. $y = x + \frac{1}{3}$

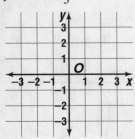

11. $y = \frac{1}{4}x + 2$

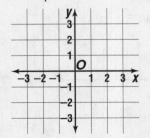

12. $y = -x$

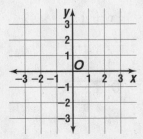

Mathematics: Applications and Connections, Course 2

7-1

Study Guide

Estimating with Fractions

Use rounding or patterns to estimate with fractions.

Rounding: | For mixed numbers, round to the nearest whole number. | For proper fractions, round to 0, $\frac{1}{2}$ or 1.

$4\frac{1}{6} + 3\frac{7}{8} \rightarrow 4 + 4 = 8$ $\qquad$ $\frac{11}{12} - \frac{4}{9} \rightarrow 1 - \frac{1}{2} = \frac{1}{2}$

$4\frac{1}{6} + 3\frac{7}{8}$ is about 8. $\qquad$ $\frac{11}{12} - \frac{4}{9}$ is about $\frac{1}{2}$.

Compatible Numbers: $\qquad$ $\frac{1}{4} \times 19\frac{1}{2} \rightarrow \frac{1}{4} \times 20 = 5$

20 is divisible by 4.

$\frac{1}{4} \times 19\frac{1}{2}$ is about 5.

$29\frac{1}{3} \div 3\frac{9}{10} \rightarrow 28 \div 4 = 7$

28 is divisible by 4.

$29\frac{1}{3} \div 3\frac{9}{10}$ is about 7.

Round each fraction to 0, $\frac{1}{2}$, or 1.

1. $\frac{7}{8}$ $\qquad$ 2. $\frac{1}{5}$ $\qquad$ 3. $\frac{11}{12}$ $\qquad$ 4. $\frac{3}{7}$ $\qquad$ 5. $\frac{4}{9}$

Round to the nearest whole number.

6. $6\frac{3}{4}$ $\qquad$ 7. $7\frac{2}{5}$ $\qquad$ 8. $4\frac{7}{9}$ $\qquad$ 9. $12\frac{2}{11}$ $\qquad$ 10. $1\frac{1}{7}$

Estimate.

11. $\frac{3}{5} + \frac{1}{4}$ $\qquad$ 12. $\frac{7}{9} - \frac{2}{5}$ $\qquad$ 13. $5\frac{1}{8} + 6\frac{9}{11}$

14. $3\frac{9}{10} - 2\frac{1}{8}$ $\qquad$ 15. $\frac{4}{5} \times \frac{7}{8}$ $\qquad$ 16. $3\frac{5}{6} \times 2\frac{1}{9}$

17. $\frac{1}{10} \times 27\frac{1}{2}$ $\qquad$ 18. $\frac{6}{7} \div \frac{11}{12}$ $\qquad$ 19. $16\frac{1}{3} \div 3\frac{7}{9}$

7-1 Practice

Estimating with Fractions

Round each fraction to 0, $\frac{1}{2}$, or 1.

1. $\frac{7}{12}$

2. $\frac{1}{8}$

3. $\frac{9}{10}$

4. $\frac{13}{14}$

5. $\frac{4}{7}$

6. $\frac{1}{10}$

Round to the nearest whole number.

7. $1\frac{7}{8}$

8. $3\frac{1}{2}$

9. $9\frac{9}{10}$

10. $5\frac{1}{7}$

11. $7\frac{1}{4}$

12. $6\frac{5}{6}$

Estimate.

13. $\frac{3}{4} + \frac{1}{9}$

14. $\frac{1}{2} \times 19$

15. $5\frac{1}{3} - \frac{1}{4}$

16. $32\frac{1}{4} \div 2\frac{1}{6}$

17. $9\frac{3}{7} - 3\frac{1}{2}$

18. $3\frac{4}{5} \times 1\frac{1}{3}$

19. $\frac{9}{10} - \frac{1}{20}$

20. $12 \div 2\frac{5}{6}$

21. $2\frac{1}{7} + 5\frac{9}{10}$

22. $\frac{1}{2} \times 19\frac{3}{4}$

23. $33\frac{1}{4} \div 3\frac{1}{6}$

24. $10\frac{1}{7} - 4\frac{1}{3}$

7-2

Study Guide

Adding and Subtracting Fractions

To add and subtract fractions, rename the fractions with a common denominator as necessary. Then add or subtract the numerators and simplify.

Examples   Add or subtract. Write each sum or difference in simplest form.

	Find the least common multiple (LCM).	Rename the fractions with a common denominator.	Add numerators. Simplify.

1 $\dfrac{7}{8}$
$+\dfrac{7}{12}$

$8 = 2 \times 2 \times 2$
$12 = 2 \times 2 \times 3$
The LCM of 8 and 12
is $2 \times 2 \times 2 \times 3$, or 24.

$\dfrac{7}{8} = \dfrac{21}{24}$
$+\dfrac{7}{12} = \dfrac{14}{24}$

$\dfrac{21}{24}$
$+\dfrac{14}{24}$
$\dfrac{35}{24} = 1\dfrac{11}{24}$

	Find the LCM.	Rename.	Subtract. Simplify.

2 $\dfrac{7}{9}$
$-\dfrac{1}{6}$

$9 = 3 \times 3$
$6 = 2 \times 3$
The LCM of 6 and 9
is $2 \times 3 \times 3$, or 18.

$\dfrac{7}{9} = \dfrac{14}{18}$
$-\dfrac{1}{6} = \dfrac{3}{18}$

$\dfrac{14}{18}$
$-\dfrac{3}{18}$
$\dfrac{11}{18}$

Add or subtract. Write each sum or difference in simplest form.

1. $\dfrac{5}{8} + \dfrac{1}{8}$

2. $\dfrac{7}{9} - \dfrac{2}{9}$

3. $\dfrac{1}{2} + \dfrac{3}{4}$

4. $\dfrac{2}{5} - \dfrac{1}{6}$

5. $\dfrac{4}{7} + \dfrac{1}{2}$

6. $\dfrac{11}{12} - \dfrac{2}{3}$

7. $\dfrac{4}{9} + \dfrac{5}{6}$

8. $\dfrac{5}{6} - \dfrac{5}{8}$

9. $\dfrac{1}{4} + \dfrac{3}{8}$

10. $\dfrac{8}{15} - \dfrac{2}{5}$

11. $\dfrac{7}{12} - \dfrac{3}{10}$

12. $\dfrac{1}{2} + \dfrac{1}{6}$

Mathematics: Applications and Connections, Course 2

7-2 Practice

Adding and Subtracting Fractions

Add or subtract. Write each sum or difference in simplest form.

1. $\frac{1}{7}$
   $+\frac{3}{7}$

2. $\frac{3}{4}$
   $-\frac{1}{4}$

3. $\frac{11}{12}$
   $-\frac{1}{3}$

4. $\frac{8}{15}$
   $-\frac{2}{5}$

5. $\frac{17}{25}$
   $+\frac{3}{10}$

6. $\frac{7}{8}$
   $+\frac{2}{3}$

7. $\frac{6}{7}$
   $-\frac{1}{7}$

8. $\frac{9}{10}$
   $+\frac{1}{5}$

9. $\frac{2}{3}$
   $+\frac{6}{7}$

10. $\frac{11}{15} + \frac{3}{5}$

11. $\frac{4}{5} - \frac{1}{10}$

12. $\frac{17}{18} - \frac{2}{9}$

13. $\frac{3}{4} + \frac{1}{9}$

14. $\frac{7}{8} - \frac{1}{3}$

15. $\frac{7}{9} + \frac{1}{3}$

16. $\frac{3}{4} - \frac{2}{5}$

17. $\frac{2}{5} + \frac{12}{13}$

18. $\frac{3}{20} + \frac{3}{10}$

Mathematics: Applications and Connections, Course 2

7-3 Study Guide

Adding and Subtracting Mixed Numbers

To add or subtract mixed number:
1. Add or subtract the fractions. Rename if necessary.
2. Add or subtract the whole numbers.
3. Rename and simplify.

Examples

1 $14\frac{1}{2}$ $\longrightarrow$ $14\frac{3}{6}$ $\longrightarrow$ $14\frac{3}{6}$ $\longrightarrow$ $14\frac{3}{6}$

   $+\ 18\frac{2}{3}$ $\quad$ $+\ 18\frac{4}{6}$ $\quad$ $+\ 18\frac{4}{6}$ $\quad$ $+\ 18\frac{4}{6}$

$\qquad\qquad\qquad\qquad\qquad\qquad\qquad\qquad\ \frac{7}{6}\qquad\qquad 32\frac{7}{6}=33\frac{1}{6}$

2 21 $\longrightarrow$ $20\frac{8}{8}$ $\longrightarrow$ $20\frac{8}{8}$ $\longrightarrow$ $20\frac{8}{8}$

   $-\ 12\frac{5}{8}$ $\quad$ $-\ 12\frac{5}{8}$ $\quad$ $-\ 12\frac{5}{8}$ $\quad$ $-\ 12\frac{5}{8}$

$\qquad\qquad\qquad\qquad\qquad\qquad\qquad\qquad\ \frac{3}{8}\qquad\qquad\quad 8\frac{3}{8}$

Complete.

1. $7\frac{1}{6}=6\frac{\square}{6}$

2. $5\frac{2}{5}=4\frac{\square}{5}$

3. $8\frac{1}{2}=7\frac{\square}{2}$

4. $9=8\frac{\square}{7}$

5. $4\frac{12}{9}=\boxed{}\frac{1}{3}$

6. $7\frac{10}{8}=8\frac{\square}{4}$

Add or subtract. Write each sum or difference in simplest form.

7. $8\frac{1}{7}+5\frac{3}{7}$

8. $9\frac{3}{4}-2\frac{1}{4}$

9. $6\frac{5}{8}+3\frac{3}{8}$

10. $5\frac{1}{2}-3\frac{1}{4}$

11. $6\frac{1}{3}+2\frac{1}{6}$

12. $9-3\frac{2}{5}$

13. $2\frac{3}{4}+7\frac{3}{4}$

14. $6\frac{1}{2}-6\frac{1}{3}$

15. $18\frac{1}{2}+5\frac{5}{8}$

16. $13\frac{2}{9}-7\frac{1}{3}$

17. $15\frac{14}{15}+13\frac{1}{2}$

18. $26-6\frac{12}{13}$

7-3 Practice

Adding and Subtracting Mixed Numbers

Complete. Use circle diagrams if necessary.

1. $3\frac{1}{3} = 2\frac{\square}{3}$

2. $9\frac{7}{5} = \boxed{}\frac{2}{5}$

3. $7\frac{1}{2} = 6\frac{\square}{2}$

4. $4\frac{9}{7} = 5\frac{\square}{7}$

5. $6\frac{7}{8} = 5\frac{\square}{8}$

6. $12\frac{3}{4} = 11\frac{\square}{4}$

Add or subtract. Write each sum or difference in simplest form.

7. $2\frac{1}{3} + 5\frac{1}{3}$

8. $9\frac{6}{7} - 6\frac{1}{7}$

9. $3\frac{4}{5} + 1\frac{3}{5}$

10. $8\frac{3}{4} - 5\frac{1}{8}$

11. $7\frac{5}{6} - 2\frac{1}{3}$

12. $9\frac{5}{12} - 5\frac{3}{4}$

13. $12\frac{7}{10} - 5\frac{3}{4}$

14. $6\frac{5}{6} + 7\frac{3}{8}$

15. $9\frac{3}{8} - 1\frac{2}{3}$

16. $10\frac{7}{9} + 4\frac{1}{4}$

17. $8\frac{4}{15} - 6\frac{3}{5}$

18. $2\frac{1}{4} + 3\frac{1}{2} + 5\frac{5}{8}$

Mathematics: Applications and Connections, Course 2

7-4 Study Guide

Multiplying Fractions and Mixed Numbers

To multiply fractions: Multiply the numerators.
Then multiply the denominators.

$$\frac{5}{6} \times \frac{3}{5} = \frac{5 \times 3}{6 \times 5} = \frac{15}{30} = \frac{1}{2}$$

To multiply mixed numbers: Rename each mixed number as a fraction.
Multiply the fractions.

$$7 \times 1\frac{1}{4} = \frac{7}{1} \times \frac{5}{4} = \frac{35}{4} = 8\frac{3}{4}$$

Multiply. Write each product in simplest form.

1. $\frac{2}{3} \times \frac{1}{4}$

2. $\frac{3}{7} \times \frac{1}{2}$

3. $\frac{1}{3} \times \frac{3}{5}$

4. $\frac{1}{2} \times \frac{6}{7}$

5. $\frac{3}{8} \times 4$

6. $\frac{7}{10} \times \frac{5}{7}$

7. $\frac{4}{9} \times 3$

8. $\frac{1}{4} \times \frac{1}{4}$

9. $1\frac{1}{2} \times 6$

10. $\frac{3}{4} \times 1\frac{2}{3}$

11. $3\frac{1}{3} \times 2\frac{1}{2}$

12. $4\frac{1}{5} \times \frac{1}{7}$

13. $1\frac{1}{9} \times \frac{3}{5}$

14. $6 \times \frac{11}{12}$

15. $\frac{1}{2} \times 2\frac{2}{3}$

7-4 Practice

Multiplying Fractions and Mixed Numbers

Multiply. Write each product in simplest form.

1. $\frac{2}{3} \times \frac{1}{2}$

2. $\frac{3}{4} \times \frac{1}{9}$

3. $3 \times \frac{4}{9}$

4. $\frac{1}{5} \times \frac{1}{4}$

5. $\frac{1}{4} \times \frac{4}{5}$

6. $\frac{4}{9} \times \frac{3}{4}$

7. $\frac{13}{21} \times \frac{7}{13}$

8. $\frac{7}{8} \times \frac{4}{9}$

9. $\frac{5}{7} \times \frac{7}{10}$

10. $\frac{4}{5} \times \frac{5}{14}$

11. $\frac{1}{4} \times \frac{5}{8}$

12. $\frac{2}{3} \times \frac{5}{9}$

13. $\frac{4}{5} \times 7$

14. $2\frac{2}{5} \times 1\frac{3}{7}$

15. $6 \times \frac{2}{3}$

16. $3\frac{3}{4} \times 12$

17. $1\frac{5}{9} \times 2\frac{4}{7}$

18. $4\frac{1}{3} \times \frac{1}{2}$

7-5 Study Guide

Integration: Measurement
Changing Customary Units

Customary Units	
Weight	**Liquid Capacity**
1 pound (lb) = 16 ounces (oz) 1 ton (T) = 2,000 pounds	1 cup (c) = 8 fluid ounces (fl oz) 1 pint (pt) = 2 cups 1 quart (qt) = 2 pints 1 gallon (1 gal) = 4 quarts

To change from larger units to smaller units, multiply.

Example 1 $5\frac{1}{2}$ lb = _____ oz   *larger unit → smaller unit*

$5\frac{1}{2} \times 16 = 88$ *Multiply to change from pounds to ounces.*

$5\frac{1}{2}$ lb = 88 oz

To change from smaller units to larger units, divide.

Example 2   **28 fl oz = _____ c**   *smaller unit → larger unit*

$28 \div 8 = 3\frac{1}{2}$ *Divide to change from quarts to gallons.*

28 fl oz = $3\frac{1}{2}$ c

Complete.

1. 4 lb = _____ oz

2. 3 T = _____ lb

3. 5 c = _____ fl oz

4. 40 oz = _____ lb

5. 5,000 lb = _____ T

6. 2 pt = _____ c

7. 1.5 lb = _____ oz

8. 10 pt = _____ qt

9. 12 qt = _____ gal

10. 2.5 pt = _____ c

11. 1.5 gal = _____ qt

12. 3.5 qt = _____ pt

13. 12 fl oz = _____ c

14. 24 oz = _____ lb

15. 7 c = _____ fl oz

16. 3 gal = _____ qt

17. 5.5 T = _____ lb

18. 48 fl oz = _____ c

7-5 Practice

Integration: Measurement
Changing Customary Units

Complete.

1. 4 lb = _____ oz

2. 12 qt = _____ gal

3. 10 c = _____ pt

4. 10,000 lb = _____ tons

5. 16 fl oz = _____ c

6. 32 oz = _____ lb

7. 5 c = _____ fl oz

8. 12 gal = _____ qt

9. 12 pt = _____ qt

10. 7 c = _____ pt

11. 5 tons = _____ lb

12. 6 gal = _____ qt

13. 3 gal = _____ qt

14. 24 pt = _____ c

15. 17 tons = _____ lb

16. 24 fl oz = _____ c

17. 9 gal = _____ qt

18. 53 qts = _____ gal

19. 9.5 tons = _____ lb

20. 15 c = _____ pt

21. 3.5 c = _____ fl oz

22. 11 c = _____ pt

23. 23 pt = _____ qt

24. 0.5 qt = _____ pt

Solve.

25. At liftoff, the space shuttle *Atlantis* weighed 100 tons. How many pounds is this?

26. The gasoline tank of a minivan holds 18 gallons. How many quarts is this?

27. The average weight of a baby at birth is 7 pounds. How many ounces is this?

28. Portable telephones can weigh as little as 8 ounces. How many pounds is this?

28. Milk is sold in 8 fl oz, 16 fl oz, 32 fl oz, and 64 fl oz cardboard containers. Change these sizes to cups.

30. The United States exports over 200 billion pounds of coal. How many tons is this?

7-6 Study Guide

Integration: Geometry
Perimeter

The distance around a geometric figure is called its **perimeter**.

To find the perimeter of a figure, add the measures of its sides.

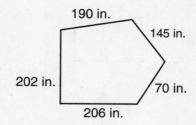

190 in.
145 in.
202 in.
70 in.
206 in.

Example 1 $P = 145 + 70 + 206 + 202 + 190$
$= 813$
The perimeter is 813 inches.

The perimeter of a rectangle equals 2 times the length plus 2 times the width.

$$P = 2\ell + 2w$$

Example 2 $P = (2 \cdot 24) + (2 \cdot 12)$
$= 48 + 24$
$= 72$
The perimeter is 72 centimeters.

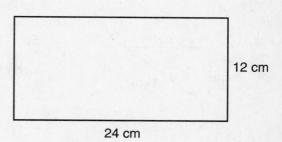

12 cm

24 cm

Find the perimeter of each figure shown or described.

1.
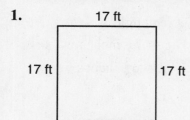
17 ft
17 ft   17 ft
17 ft

2.
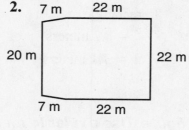
7 m   22 m
20 m   22 m
7 m   22 m

3.
$2\frac{1}{2}$ in. $2\frac{3}{10}$ in.
$2\frac{3}{10}$ in. $2\frac{1}{2}$ in.

4.
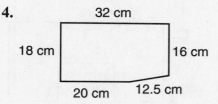
32 cm
18 cm   16 cm
20 cm   12.5 cm

5.
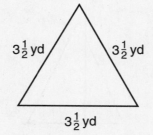
$3\frac{1}{2}$ yd $3\frac{1}{2}$ yd
$3\frac{1}{2}$ yd

6.
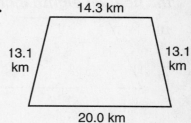
14.3 km
13.1 km   13.1 km
20.0 km

7. rectangle:
$\ell = 8$ feet
$w = 5$ feet

8. rectangle:
$\ell = 3.5$ meters
$w = 2$ meters

9. rectangle:
$\ell = 17$ yards
$w = 8.5$ yards

7-6 Practice

Integration: Geometry
Perimeter

Find the perimeter of each figure shown or described.

1.
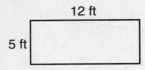
12 ft

5 ft

2.
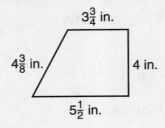
$3\frac{3}{4}$ in.

$4\frac{3}{8}$ in.

4 in.

$5\frac{1}{2}$ in.

3.
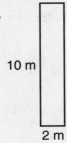
10 m

2 m

4.
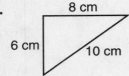
8 cm

6 cm

10 cm

5.
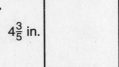
$4\frac{3}{5}$ in.

6.
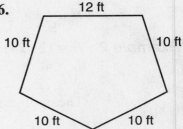
12 ft

10 ft   10 ft

10 ft   10 ft

7. rectangle:
$\ell = 6$ yards
$w = 4$ yards

8. rectangle:
$\ell = 8.2$ meters
$w = 7.1$ meters

9. rectangle:
$\ell = 7\frac{1}{2}$ inches
$w = 6\frac{3}{8}$ inches

Find the perimeter of each figure. Use a ruler to measure to the nearest eighth inch.

10.
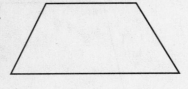

11.
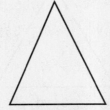

12.
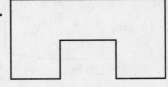

13. Find the perimeter of a square with side $14\frac{1}{2}$ inches.

14. Find the perimeter of a triangle with sides 4 inches, $8\frac{1}{2}$ inches, and $9\frac{1}{4}$ inches.

7- Study Guide

Integration: Measurement
Circles and Circumference

A **circle** is the set of all points in a plane that are the same distance from a given point called the **center**.

The **diameter (*d*)** is the distance across the circle through its center.

The **radius (*r*)** is the distance from the center to any point on the circle.

The **circumference (*C*)** is the distance around the circle.

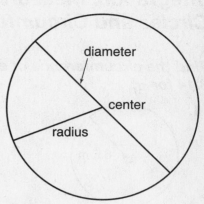

Examples

1 **Find the circumference of a circle with a diameter of 7.5 inches.**

$C = \pi d$
$C \approx 3.14 \times 7.5$ *Use 3.14 for π.*
$C \approx 23.55$ The circumference of the circle is about 23.55 inches.

2 **If the radius of a circle is 14 inches, what is its circumference?**

$C = 2\pi r$
$C \approx 2 \times \frac{22}{7} \times 14$ *Use $\frac{22}{7}$ for π.*
$C \approx 88$ The circumference of the circle is about 88 inches.

Find the circumference of each circle to the nearest tenth. Use $\frac{22}{7}$ or 3.14 for π.

1.	2.	3.	4.

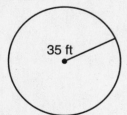 35 ft

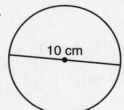 10 cm

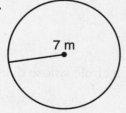 7 m

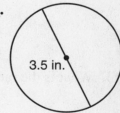 3.5 in.

5. $d = 21$ km   **6.** $r = 42$ mi   **7.** $d = 68$ m   **8.** $r = 700$ ft

9. $r = 91$ cm   **10.** $d = 5$ km   **11.** $r = 90$ ft   **12.** $d = 6.3$ m

7-7 Practice

Integration: Measurement
Circles and Circumference

Find the circumference of each circle to the nearest tenth. Use 3.14 for π.

1.

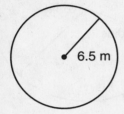

6.5 m

2.

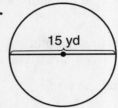

15 yd

3.

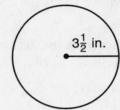

$3\frac{1}{2}$ in.

4.

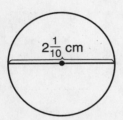

$2\frac{1}{10}$ cm

5.

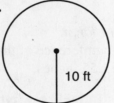

10 ft

6.

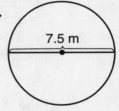

7.5 m

7. $d = 8\frac{3}{4}$ in.

8. $d = 11.5$ cm

9. $r = 11$ ft

10. $r = 6.8$ m

11. $r = 4\frac{2}{3}$ ft

12. $d = 2\frac{1}{3}$ yd

13. What is the radius of a circle whose diameter is 8 meters long?

14. What is the diameter of a circle whose radius is 20.4 centimeters long?

7-8 Study Guide

Properties

The table shows the properties for addition and multiplication of fractions.

Property	Examples
Commutative The sum or product of two fractions is the same regardless of the order in which they are added or multiplied.	$\frac{1}{2} + \frac{1}{4} = \frac{1}{4} + \frac{1}{2}$ $\frac{2}{3} \times \frac{1}{5} = \frac{1}{5} \times \frac{2}{3}$
Associative The sum or product of three or more fractions is the same regardless of the way in which they are grouped.	$\left(\frac{1}{2} + \frac{5}{6}\right) + \frac{7}{8} = \frac{1}{2} + \left(\frac{5}{6} + \frac{7}{8}\right)$ $\frac{1}{8} \times \left(\frac{3}{4} \times \frac{6}{7}\right) = \left(\frac{1}{8} \times \frac{3}{4}\right) \times \frac{6}{7}$
Identity The sum of any fraction and 0 is the fraction. The product of any fraction and 1 is the fraction.	$\frac{7}{8} + 0 = \frac{7}{8}$ $\frac{5}{9} \times 1 = \frac{5}{9}$
Inverse (Reciprocal) The product of a fraction and its reciprocal is 1.	$\frac{7}{8} \times \frac{8}{7} = 1$
Distributive The sum of two fractions multiplied by a number is equal to the sum of the products of each fraction and the number.	$\frac{2}{3}\left(\frac{1}{2} + \frac{3}{7}\right) = \left(\frac{2}{3} \times \frac{1}{2}\right) + \left(\frac{2}{3} \times \frac{3}{7}\right)$

Name the property shown by each statement.

1. $\frac{11}{12} \times 1 = \frac{11}{12}$

2. $\left(\frac{1}{5} + \frac{2}{3}\right) + \frac{5}{9} = \frac{1}{5} + \left(\frac{2}{3} + \frac{5}{9}\right)$

3. $\frac{3}{4} \times \frac{5}{6} = \frac{5}{6} \times \frac{3}{4}$

4. $\frac{3}{5} \times \left(\frac{1}{3} + \frac{5}{7}\right) = \left(\frac{3}{5} \times \frac{1}{3}\right) + \left(\frac{3}{5} \times \frac{5}{7}\right)$

5. $\frac{9}{4} \times \frac{4}{9} = 1$

6. $\frac{4}{5} + \frac{3}{4} = \frac{3}{4} + \frac{4}{5}$

7. $0 + \frac{17}{18} = \frac{17}{18}$

8. $\frac{2}{9} \times \left(\frac{1}{4} \times \frac{9}{10}\right) = \left(\frac{2}{9} \times \frac{1}{4}\right) \times \frac{9}{10}$

Name the multiplicative inverse of each number.

9. $\frac{6}{11}$

10. $\frac{19}{3}$

11. $\frac{1}{8}$

12. 9

7-8 Practice

Properties

Name the property shown by each statement.

1. $\frac{3}{8} + 0 = \frac{3}{8}$

2. $\frac{3}{4} \times \left(\frac{1}{2} \times \frac{1}{3}\right) = \left(\frac{3}{4} \times \frac{1}{2}\right) \times \frac{1}{3}$

3. $\frac{1}{3} \times \left(\frac{1}{4} + \frac{3}{5}\right) = \frac{1}{3} \times \frac{1}{4} + \frac{1}{3} \times \frac{3}{5}$

4. $\frac{3}{5} + \frac{5}{9} = \frac{5}{9} + \frac{3}{5}$

5. $\frac{1}{6} \times \frac{3}{4} = \frac{3}{4} \times \frac{1}{6}$

6. $1\frac{7}{9} \times 1 = 1\frac{7}{9}$

Name the multiplicative inverse of each number.

7. 5

8. $1\frac{3}{4}$

9. $\frac{7}{9}$

10. 1

11. $2\frac{1}{2}$

12. $\frac{3}{13}$

Solve each equation. Write the solution in simplest form.

13. $\frac{3}{2}h = 6$

14. $3 \times 1\frac{1}{5} = p$

15. $7\frac{1}{10} \times 8 = d$

Compute mentally.

16. $\frac{1}{2} \times 6\frac{2}{7}$

17. $9\frac{9}{24} \times \frac{1}{3}$

18. $8\frac{4}{9} \times \frac{1}{4}$

7-9 Study Guide

Dividing Fractions and Mixed Numbers

To divide fractions and mixed numbers:
1. Write any mixed numbers as improper fractions.
2. Find the reciprocal of the divisor.
3. Multiply the dividend by the reciprocal of the divisor.

Examples **1** $\frac{5}{8} \div \frac{5}{12}$ *The reciprocal of $\frac{5}{12}$ is $\frac{12}{5}$.*

$$\frac{5}{8} \div \frac{5}{12} = \frac{5}{8} \times \frac{12}{5}$$

$$= \frac{60}{40} \text{ or } 1\frac{1}{2}$$

2 $7 \div 3\frac{1}{2} \rightarrow \frac{7}{1} \div \frac{7}{2}$ *The reciprocal of $\frac{7}{2}$ is $\frac{2}{7}$.*

$$7 \div 3\frac{1}{2} = \frac{7}{1} \times \frac{2}{7}$$

$$= \frac{14}{7} \text{ or } 2$$

Name the reciprocal of each number.

1. $\frac{6}{11}$ **2.** $\frac{14}{5}$ **3.** 8   **4.** $\frac{1}{5}$

Divide. Write each quotient in simplest form.

5. $n = \frac{7}{8} \div \frac{1}{4}$ **6.** $p = \frac{2}{5} \div \frac{5}{8}$ **7.** $y = \frac{1}{3} \div \frac{1}{6}$

8. $8 \div \frac{1}{3} = k$ **9.** $\frac{5}{9} \div 5 = v$ **10.** $24 \div 1\frac{1}{2} = t$

11. $c = 2\frac{1}{2} \div 5$ **12.** $z = 3\frac{1}{3} \div \frac{2}{9}$ **13.** $m = \frac{5}{8} \div 2\frac{1}{2}$

14. $1\frac{1}{3} \div 2\frac{1}{2} = t$ **15.** $3\frac{1}{3} \div 1\frac{2}{5} = f$ **16.** $\frac{9}{10} \div 5\frac{2}{5} = k$

7-9 Practice

Dividing Fractions and Mixed Numbers

Divide. Write each quotient in simplest form.

1. $\frac{7}{8} \div \frac{2}{3}$

2. $5 \div \frac{3}{5}$

3. $3\frac{1}{4} \div 2\frac{1}{3}$

Solve each equation.

4. $s = \frac{3}{4} \div \frac{1}{2}$

5. $k = \frac{4}{5} \div \frac{1}{3}$

6. $\frac{1}{5} \div \frac{1}{4} = y$

7. $u = 4 \div \frac{1}{3}$

8. $\frac{4}{7} \div \frac{8}{9} = j$

9. $w = \frac{3}{8} \div \frac{3}{4}$

10. $\frac{9}{7} \div \frac{3}{14} = h$

11. $\frac{4}{5} \div \frac{2}{5} = p$

12. $5 \div 3\frac{3}{4} = q$

13. $c = \frac{3}{8} \div 2\frac{1}{4}$

14. $t = 7\frac{1}{3} \div 4$

15. $m = 3\frac{1}{4} \div 2\frac{1}{4}$

16. $n = 1\frac{2}{7} \div 1\frac{13}{14}$

17. $1\frac{1}{5} \div \frac{3}{10} = r$

18. $7\frac{1}{2} \div 2\frac{5}{6} = w$

8-1 Study Guide

Ratios

A **ratio** is a comparison of two numbers by division.

Example 1   Ron made 10 out of 16 foul shots. Write a ratio of the shots Ron made to his total shots.

The ratio of foul shots made to total foul shots is:

10 to 16, 10:16, or $\frac{10}{16}$.

Since a ratio can be written as a fraction, ratios are often written in simplest form.

foul shots made $\rightarrow$ $\frac{10}{16} = \frac{\overset{5}{\cancel{10}}}{\underset{8}{\cancel{16}}}$ or $\frac{5}{8}$
total foul shots $\rightarrow$

The ratio can also be expressed as a decimal: $10 \div 16 = 0.625$.

Two ratios are equivalent if the simplest form of the ratios are equal.

Example 2   Tell whether 12:18 and 14:21 are equivalent ratios.

Express each ratio as a fraction in simplest form.

$\frac{12}{18} = \frac{12 \div 6}{18 \div 6} = \frac{2}{3}$ $\frac{14}{21} = \frac{14 \div 7}{21 \div 7} = \frac{2}{3}$

Since $\frac{2}{3} = \frac{2}{3}$, the ratios are equivalent.

Express each ratio as a fraction in simplest form.

1. 16 to 20

2. 35:40

3. 27 feet to 24 feet

4. 13 hours:52 hours

5. 25 to 90

6. 45 minutes to 75 minutes

7. 2 hours:1 day

8. 96:18

9. $\frac{24}{40}$

Tell whether the ratios are equivalent. Show your answer by simplifying.

10. $\frac{64}{80}$ and $\frac{20}{25}$

11. 42 to 49 and 54 to 63

12. 18:42 and 20:44

13. 35 to 15 and 49 to 21

14. 144:36 and 72:32

15. 16 to 96 and 1 to 6

Mathematics: Applications and Connections, Course 2

8-1 Practice

Ratios

Express each ratio as a fraction in simplest form.

1. $\frac{6}{8}$

2. 9 to 15

3. 32:6

4. 6 pounds:12 ounces

5. 14 hours to 3 days

6. 3 yards:8 feet

7. 12 to 40

8. 68:18

9. 3 hours to 88 minutes

10. 32:15

11. 8 weeks out of 14 weeks

12. 29 inches to 58 inches

Tell whether the ratios in each pair are equivalent. Show your answer by simplifying.

13. $\frac{35}{50}$ and $\frac{7}{5}$

14. $\frac{9}{10}$ and $\frac{180}{200}$

15. $\frac{75}{5}$ and $\frac{25}{1}$

16. 8:4 and 36:20

17. 3 pounds:12 ounces and
    6 pounds:24 ounces

18. 6 hours to 4 days and
    12 hours to 10 days

19. 12 to 60 and 100 to 500

20. 32 minutes to 72 minutes and
    90 minutes to 40 minutes

8-2 Study Guide

Rates

A **rate** is a ratio of two measurements with different units.

Example 1   **Six bottles of mineral water cost $2.59.**

        The ratio 6 bottles for $2.59 is a rate.

A rate in which the denominator is 1 is a **unit rate.**

Example 2   **Express 6 bottles for $2.59 as a unit rate.**

$$\begin{array}{l} price \rightarrow \\ bottles \rightarrow \end{array} \frac{\$2.59}{6} = \frac{\$2.59 \div 6}{6 \div 6}$$

$$\approx \frac{\$0.4317}{1}$$

        The unit rate is about $0.43 per bottle.

Express each rate as a unit rate.

1. 120 miles in 3 hours

2. 72 apples for 12 people

3. $1 for 3 pounds of bananas

4. 36 breaths in 3 minutes

5. $1.69 for 12 muffins

6. 45 kilometers in 5 hours

7. 352 steps in 4 minutes

8. $9.96 for 6 roses

9. 279 students for 9 teachers

10. 1,520 people in 5 square miles

11. $450 for 6 days

12. 7 inches of rain in 4 days

8-2 Practice

Rates

Express each rate as a unit rate.

1. $3.24 for 3 pounds

2. $75 for 6 compact discs

3. 100 people in 4 rows

4. 2.5 pounds for $7.50

5. $900 for 5 days

6. 14 pounds in 7 weeks

7. 385 miles in 7 hours

8. $47.00 for 4 shirts

9. 4 cups for 3 recipes

10. 2,500 tickets in 10 days

11. 9 cups for 3 pounds

12. 12 ounces for 3 cups

13. 18 people in 6 cars

14. $32.00 for 10 floppy disks

15. $14.00 for 7 minutes

16. $12.00 for 3 hours

17. The Main Street Market sells oranges at $3.00 for five pounds and
apples at $3.99 for three pounds. The Off Street Market sells oranges
at $2.59 for four pounds and apples at $1.98 for two pounds.
a. Find the unit price for each item at each store.

b. Which store has the better buy for oranges? for apples?

*Mathematics: Applications
and Connections, Course 2*

8-3 Study Guide

Solving Proportions

A **proportion** is an equation that shows that two ratios are equivalent. The **cross products** of a proportion are equal. If one term of a proportion is not known, you can use cross products to find the term. This is called **solving the proportion.**

Example 1 Solve $\frac{2}{3} = \frac{f}{18}$.

$$\frac{2}{3} = \frac{f}{18}$$

$2 \times 18 = 3 \times f$ *Find the cross products.*

$36 = 3f$

$\frac{36}{3} = \frac{3f}{3}$ *Divide each side by 3.*

$12 = f$

Example 2 Solve $\frac{r}{24} = \frac{7}{8}$.

$$\frac{r}{24} = \frac{7}{8}$$

$r \times 8 = 24 \times 7$ *Find the cross products.*

$8r = 168$

$\frac{8r}{8} = \frac{168}{8}$ *Divide each side by 8.*

$r = 21$

Solve each proportion.

1. $\frac{2}{n} = \frac{5}{10}$

2. $\frac{5}{8} = \frac{m}{24}$

3. $\frac{12}{20} = \frac{k}{15}$

4. $\frac{y}{7} = \frac{7}{49}$

5. $\frac{21}{f} = \frac{9}{12}$

6. $\frac{10}{12} = \frac{15}{v}$

7. $\frac{3.5}{m} = \frac{16}{32}$

8. $\frac{6}{20} = \frac{n}{50}$

9. $\frac{75}{r} = \frac{6}{2}$

10. $\frac{f}{0.8} = \frac{2}{8}$

11. $\frac{15}{120} = \frac{t}{16}$

12. $\frac{7}{9} = \frac{c}{36}$

8-3 Practice

Solving Proportions

Solve each proportion.

1. $\dfrac{n}{8} = \dfrac{12}{16}$

2. $\dfrac{3}{k} = \dfrac{5}{15}$

3. $\dfrac{18}{30} = \dfrac{v}{4}$

4. $\dfrac{2.8}{4} = \dfrac{7}{x}$

5. $\dfrac{r}{5} = \dfrac{65}{75}$

6. $\dfrac{18}{m} = \dfrac{3}{36}$

7. $\dfrac{24}{13} = \dfrac{b}{26}$

8. $\dfrac{300}{24} = \dfrac{18}{j}$

9. $\dfrac{w}{5} = \dfrac{25}{1,000}$

10. $\dfrac{0.24}{a} = \dfrac{3}{9.6}$

11. $\dfrac{17}{8.5} = \dfrac{z}{0.01}$

12. $\dfrac{8}{45} = \dfrac{80}{q}$

13. $\dfrac{0.1}{8.2} = \dfrac{1.8}{a}$

14. $\dfrac{4.2}{b} = \dfrac{8}{5}$

15. $\dfrac{c}{5} = \dfrac{650}{6.5}$

16. Josh spends 40 cents out of every dollar on snacks, 14 cents out of every dollar on school supplies, and saves the rest. If Josh earns $32.00 per week cutting lawns, how much does he save per week?

8-4 Study Guide

Scale Drawings

A **scale drawing** is used to present something that is too large or too small to be drawn to actual size. The **scale** is the ratio of the distance on the drawing to the actual distance.

Example   Chuck is making a scale drawing of Detroit's Tiger Stadium. He is using the scale $\frac{1}{4}$ inch:25 feet. The home-run distance from home plate to right field is 325 feet. What length should Chuck make this distance on his drawing?

Use the scale $\frac{1}{4}$ inch:25 feet. Solve a proportion.

$$\begin{array}{l} \textit{drawing length} \longrightarrow \\ \textit{actual length} \longrightarrow \end{array} \frac{\frac{1}{4}}{25} = \frac{x}{325} \begin{array}{l} \longleftarrow \textit{drawing length} \\ \longleftarrow \textit{actual length} \end{array}$$

$$\frac{1}{4} \times 325 = 25x \qquad \textit{Find cross products.}$$
$$81\frac{1}{4} = 25x$$
$$\frac{81\frac{1}{4}}{25} = \frac{25x}{25}$$
$$3\frac{1}{4} = x$$

On Chuck's drawing, the length should be $3\frac{1}{4}$ inches.

On a map, the scale is 1 inch:160 miles. For each map distance, find the actual distance.

1. 3 inches
2. $1\frac{1}{2}$ inches
3. $2\frac{5}{8}$ inches
4. $4\frac{1}{4}$ inches

5. $2\frac{3}{4}$ inches
6. 7 inches
7. $1\frac{7}{8}$ inches
8. $5\frac{1}{2}$ inches

On a scale drawing, the scale is $\frac{1}{2}$ inch:1 foot. Find the dimensions of each room in the scale drawing.

9. 10 feet by 20 feet
10. 15 feet by 12 feet

11. 14 feet by 11 feet
12. 9 feet by 13 feet

8-4 **Practice**

Scale Drawings

On a map, the scale is 1 inch:150 miles. For each map distance, find the actual distance.

1. 3 inches

2. 8 inches

3. $\frac{3}{4}$ inch

4. $1\frac{5}{8}$ inches

5. $3\frac{1}{2}$ inches

6. $\frac{1}{4}$ inch

On a scale drawing, the scale is $\frac{1}{4}$ inch:1 foot. Find the dimensions of each room in the scale drawing.

7. 15 feet by 25 feet

8. 20 feet by 12 feet

9. 10 feet by 9 feet

10. 14 feet by 14 feet

11. 8 feet by 14 feet

12. 28 feet by 18 feet

13. On a scale drawing, 1 centimeter represents 4 meters. What length on the drawing would be used to represent 6.5 meters?

14. On a scale drawing, 1 inch represents 8 feet. What are the dimensions on the scale drawing that represent a 32 feet by 24 feet room?

8-5 Study Guide

Percents and Fractions

To write a fraction as a percent, use a proportion.

Examples   **1**   Express $\frac{5}{8}$ as a percent.   **2**   Express $\frac{15}{16}$ as a percent.

$$\frac{5}{8} = \frac{x}{100}$$ $$\frac{15}{16} = \frac{m}{100}$$

$$500 = 8x$$ $$1{,}500 = 16m$$

$$\frac{500}{8} = \frac{8x}{8}$$ $$\frac{1{,}500}{16} = \frac{16m}{16}$$

$$62.5 = x$$ $$93.75 = m$$

$\frac{5}{8}$ is 62.5%. $\frac{15}{16}$ is 93.75%.

To write a percent as a fraction, write a fraction with a denominator of 100. Then write the fraction is simplest form.

Examples   **3**   Express 24% as a fraction.   **4**   Express $87\frac{1}{2}$% as a fraction.

$$24\% = \frac{24}{100}$$ $$87\frac{1}{2}\% = \frac{87\frac{1}{2}}{100}$$

$$= \frac{24 \div 4}{100 \div 4}$$ $$= \frac{\frac{175}{2}}{100}$$

$$= \frac{6}{25}$$ $$= \frac{175}{2} \times \frac{1}{100}$$

$$= \frac{175}{200}$$

$$= \frac{7}{8}$$

Express each fraction as a percent.

1. $\frac{1}{2}$ **2.** $\frac{3}{5}$ **3.** $\frac{7}{10}$ **4.** $\frac{9}{20}$

5. $\frac{19}{25}$ **6.** $\frac{1}{8}$ **7.** $\frac{1}{6}$ **8.** $\frac{3}{4}$

Express each percent as a fraction in simplest form.

9. 40%   **10.** 30%   **11.** 85%   **12.** 56%

13. $37\frac{1}{2}$%   **14.** $33\frac{1}{3}$%   **15.** 4%   **16.** 17%

                                       Mathematics: Applications and Connections, Course 2

8-5 Practice

Percents and Fractions

Express each fraction as a percent.

1. $\frac{7}{10}$

2. $\frac{3}{4}$

3. $\frac{17}{20}$

4. $\frac{5}{8}$

5. $\frac{5}{5}$

6. $\frac{23}{25}$

7. $\frac{11}{12}$

8. $\frac{13}{16}$

9. $\frac{64}{125}$

10. $\frac{37}{50}$

11. $\frac{1}{3}$

12. $\frac{9}{16}$

Express each percent as a fraction in simplest form.

13. 75%

14. 84%

15. 90%

16. $18\frac{1}{2}\%$

17. 38%

18. $87\frac{1}{2}\%$

19. 32%

20. $8\frac{2}{3}\%$

21. 68%

22. 14%

23. $6\frac{1}{4}\%$

24. 48%

25. 56%

26. 30%

27. $2\frac{1}{2}\%$

8-6 Study Guide

Percents and Decimals

To write a decimal as a percent, multiply the decimal by 100 and add the percent symbol.

Examples **1** **Express 0.77 as a percent.**   **2** **Express 0.323 as a percent.**

$$0.77 = 0.77$$
$$= 77\%$$

$$0.323 = 0.323$$
$$= 32.3\%$$

To write a percent as a decimal, divide the percent by 100 and remove the percent symbol.

Examples **3** **Express 51% as a decimal.**   **4** **Express 90.2% as a decimal.**

$$51\% = 51.$$
$$= 0.51$$

$$90.2\% = 90.2$$
$$= 0.902$$

Express each decimal as a percent.

1. 0.67   **2.** 0.14   **3.** 0.2   **4.** 0.345

5. 0.09   **6.** 0.084   **7.** 0.02   **8.** 0.89

Express each percent as a decimal.

9. 95%   **10.** 12%   **11.** 4%   **12.** 100%

13. 14.4%   **14.** 80%   **15.** 7.5%   **16.** $10\frac{1}{2}\%$

     Mathematics: Applications and Connections, Course 2

Practice

Percents and Decimals

Express each decimal as a percent.

1. 0.52   **2.** 0.9   **3.** 0.12

4. 0.19   **5.** 0.312   **6.** 0.74

7. 0.825   **8.** 0.06   **9.** 0.066

10. 0.628   **11.** 0.4   **12.** 0.02

13. 0.537   **14.** 0.22   **15.** 0.3

Express each percent as a decimal.

16. 82%   **17.** 61.5%   **18.** 8.9%

19. 37%   **20.** 2.2%   **21.** 8%

22. 1.8%   **23.** 1.4%   **24.** 2%

25. 13%   **26.** 18%   **27.** 19.6%

28. $48\frac{1}{2}\%$ **29.** 70%   **30.** $27\frac{1}{4}\%$

8-7 Study Guide

Percents Greater Than 100% and Percents Less Than 1%

You can express a percent greater than 100% or less than 1% as a decimal.

Examples **1** **Express 725% as a decimal.** **2** **Express 0.015% as a decimal.**

$$725\% = 725$$
$$= 7.25$$

$$0.015\% = 00.015$$
$$= 0.00015$$

You can use percents to represent numbers that are greater than 1.

Examples **3** **Express 5.75 as a percent.** **4** **Express $8\frac{9}{10}$ as a percent.**

$$5.75 = 5.75$$
$$= 575\%$$

$$8\frac{9}{10} = 8.9$$
$$= 8.90$$
$$= 890\%$$

You can use percents to represent numbers that are less than 0.01 or $\frac{1}{100}$.

Examples **5** **Express 0.007 as a percent.** **6** **Express $\frac{1}{400}$ as a percent.**

$$0.007 = 0.007$$
$$= 0.7\%$$

$$\frac{1}{400} = 1 \div 400$$
$$= 0.0025$$
$$= 0.0025$$
$$= 0.25\%$$

Express each percent as a decimal.

1. 115%   **2.** 300%   **3.** 540%   **4.** 758%

5. 0.2%   **6.** 0.57%   **7.** 0.125%   **8.** 0.0006%

Express each number as a percent.

9. 5.79   **10.** $4\frac{1}{2}$ **11.** 2.4   **12.** 95

13. 0.001   **14.** $\frac{6}{1,200}$ **15.** 0.0016   **16.** $\frac{4}{1,600}$

8-7 Practice

Percents Greater Than 100% and Percents Less Than 1%

Express each percent as a decimal.

1. 520%

2. 140%

3. 235%

4. 0.32%

5. 0.015%

6. $\frac{1}{4}$%

7. $\frac{2}{5}$%

8. 1,000%

9. 0.125%

10. 240%

11. 550%

12. 8,200%

Express each number as a percent.

13. 3.4

14. 0.0026

15. $3\frac{1}{5}$

16. 1.9

17. 8

18. 0.0002

19. 1

20. 1.95

21. 35

22. 0.00112

23. 63

24. $5\frac{3}{4}$

8-8

Study Guide

Percent of a Number

A **percent** is a ratio that compares a number to 100.

Example 1 **3 out of 4 is what percent?**

$$\frac{3}{4} = \frac{r}{100}$$

$3 \times 100 = 4r$ *Find the cross products.*

$$\frac{300}{4} = \frac{4r}{4}$$ *Divide each side by 4.*

$75 = r$

3 out of 4 is 75%.

Examples **2** **What number is 20% of 180?**   **3** **40% of 48 is what number?**

Let n represent the number.   Let n represent the number.

$$\frac{n}{180} = \frac{20}{100}$$ $$\frac{n}{48} = \frac{40}{100}$$

$n \cdot 100 = 180 \cdot 20$ *Find the cross products.* $n \cdot 100 = 48 \cdot 40$

$$\frac{100n}{100} = \frac{3,600}{100}$$ *Divide each side by 100.* $$\frac{100n}{100} = \frac{1,920}{100}$$

$n = 36$ $n = 19.2$

20% of 180 is 36.   40% of 48 is 19.2.

Find each number. Round to the nearest tenth if necessary.

1. What number is 10% of 230?   **2.** 25% of 38 is what number?

4. Find 15% of 160.   **5.** What number is 24% of 20?

7. 50% of 74 is what number?   **8.** What number is 40% of 250?

10. 36% of 75 is what number?   **11.** 36% of 18 is what number?

13. What is 15% of 200?   **14.** Find 19% of 87.

16. Find 725% of 3.4.   **17.** What is 0.05% of 2999?

8-8 Practice

Percent of a Number

Find each number. Round to the nearest tenth if necessary.

1. What number is 18% of 450?

2. Find 92% of 120.

3. $37\frac{1}{2}$ is 30% of what number?

4. 45% of 156 is what number?

5. 96 is 30% of what number?

6. Forty percent of 80 is what number?

7. What number is 58% of 200?

8. $33\frac{1}{3}$% of 249 is what number?

9. What number is 12% of 150?

10. Find $82\frac{1}{2}$% of 400.

11. What number is 72% of 1,024?

12. Find 12% of 12.

13. What number is 60% of 264?

14. 96% of 72 is what number?

15. 380% of 30 is what number?

16. $37\frac{1}{2}$% of 18 is what number?

17. Find 70% of 1,760.

18. What number is 24% of 294?

8-9 Study Guide

The Percent Proportion

Use the percent proportion to solve problems.

$\frac{P}{B} = \frac{r}{100}$, where P = percentage, B = base, and $\frac{r}{100}$ = rate.

Examples

1 **12 is what percent of 96?**

$$\frac{P}{B} = \frac{r}{100}$$ *Replace P with 12 and B with 96.*

$$\frac{12}{96} = \frac{r}{100}$$

$$12 \times 100 = 96r$$ *Find the cross products.*

$$\frac{1,200}{96} = \frac{96r}{96}$$

$$12.5 = r$$

So, 12 is 12.5% of 96.

2 **What number is 120% of 55?**

$$\frac{P}{B} = \frac{r}{100}$$ *Replace B with 55 and r with 120.*

$$\frac{P}{55} = \frac{120}{100}$$

$$100P = 55 \times 120$$ *Find the cross products.*

$$\frac{100P}{100} = \frac{6,600}{100}$$

$$P = 66$$

So, 66 is 120% of 55.

Find each number. Round to the nearest tenth if necessary.

1. 12 is what percent of 14?

2. 50% of what number is 9?

3. What percent of 50 is 75?

4. Find 12.5% of 16.

5. What percent of 80 is 16?

6. 40% of what number is 32?

7. Find 90% of 68.

8. 72 is what percent of 60?

9. What number is 75% of 128?

10. $12\frac{1}{2}$ percent of what number is 2?

Practice

The Percent Proportion

Find each number. Round to the nearest tenth if necessary.

1. 12 is what percent of 30?

2. 40% of what number is 82?

3. What percent of 49 is 7?

4. 6.25% of 190 is what number?

5. 64.2% of 84 is what number?

6. What percent of 76 is 14?

7. What number is 32% of 1,000?

8. What is 84% of 180?

9. $12\frac{1}{2}$ is 25% of what number?

10. 85% of 190 is what number?

11. What percent of 128 is 24?

12. 25 is what percent of 365?

13. What number is 20% of 625?

14. $33\frac{1}{3}$% of 900 is what number?

15. 40% of what number is 36?

16. 8.25% of 180 is what number?

17. 73 is 20% of what number?

18. What percent of 185 is 35?

19. What number is 36% of 96?

20. 56% of 109 is what number?

Name _____ **Date** _____

Study Guide

9-1

Angles

An **angle** is formed by two rays with a common endpoint. The endpoint is called the **vertex** of the angle.

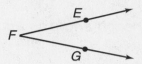

Types of Angles and Their Measures:

$\angle F$, or $\angle EFG$, or $\angle GFE$

| **right angle** | **straight angle** | **acute angle** | **obtuse angle** |

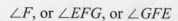
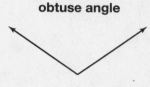

exactly 90°   exactly 180°   less than 90°   between 90° and 180°

When two angles have the same measure, they are congruent angles.

$\angle A \cong \angle B$

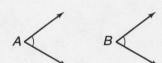

$\cong$ means _is congruent to._

Classify each angle as acute, obtuse, right, or straight.

1.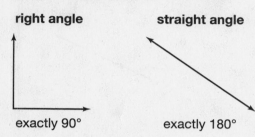

2.

3.

4. 180° angle

5. 94° angle

6. 26° angle

7.

8.

9.

9-1 Practice

Angles

Classify each angle as acute, obtuse, right or straight.

1.

2.

3.

4.

5.

6.

7. 84°

8. 179°

9. 90°

10. 180°

11. 12°

12. 91°

Classify each pair of angles as supplementary, complementary, or neither.

13.

14.

15.

16.

67

Mathematics: Applications and Connections, Course 2

9-2

Study Guide

Polygons

A **polygon** is a closed figure in a plane that:
* has at least three sides, all of which are segments,
* has sides that meet only at a vertex, and
* has exactly two sides meeting at each vertex.

These figures are polygons.

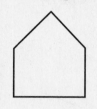     

pentagon	hexagon	heptagon	octagon	nonagon	decagon	dodecagon
5 angles	6 angles	7 angles	8 angles	9 angles	10 angles	12 angles

These figures are *not* polygons.

  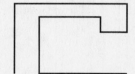

Some sides meet at places other than vertices.

Not every side is a segment.

This is not a closed figure.

Determine which figures are polygons. If the figure is a polygon, name it and tell whether it is a regular polygon. If a figure is not a polygon, explain why.

1.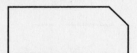

2.

3.

4.

5.

6.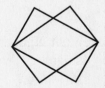

Mathematics: Applications and Connections, Course 2

9-2 Practice

Polygons

Determine which figures are polygons. If the figure is a polygon, name it and tell whether it is a regular polygon. If a figure is not a polygon, explain why.

1.

2.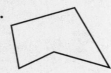

3.

4.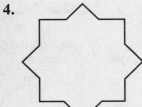

5.

6.

7.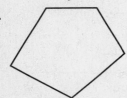

8.

9.

10.

11.

12.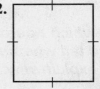

13.

14.

15.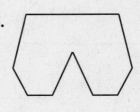

16. Draw a regular eight-sided polygon. What is its name?

17. Draw a decagon.

9-3

Study Guide

Integration: Algebra
Similar Polygons

Two polygons are **similar** if corresponding angles are congruent and corresponding sides are in proportion. The symbol ~ means "is similar to."

Example 1 △QRS ~ △ABC

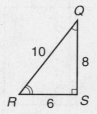

Corresponding angles are congruent:

$\angle Q = \angle A$
$\angle R = \angle B$
$\angle S = \angle C$

Corresponding sides are in proportion:

$\frac{5}{10} = \frac{4}{8} = \frac{3}{6}$

You can use proportions to find the missing length of a side in a pair of similar polygons.

Example 2 If *KLMN* ~ *WXYZ*, find the length of $\overline{MN}$.

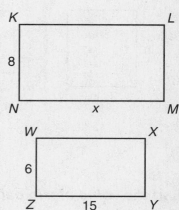

$\begin{array}{l} \overline{KN} \to \\ \overline{WZ} \to \end{array} \frac{8}{6} = \frac{x}{15} \begin{array}{l} \leftarrow \overline{MN} \\ \leftarrow \overline{YZ} \end{array}$

$8 \times 15 = 68$ *Find the cross products.*
$120 = 6x$
$20 = x$

The length of $\overline{MN}$ is 20.

Tell whether each pair of polygons is similar.

1.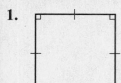

2.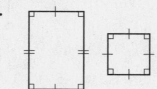

3.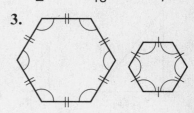

Find the value of x in each pair of similar polygons.

4.

5.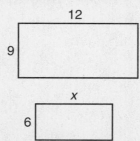

6.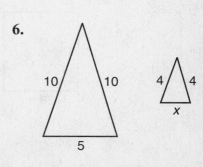

Mathematics: Applications and Connections, Course 2

Practice

Integration: Algebra
Similar Polygons

Tell whether each pair of polygons is similar. Justify your answer.

1.

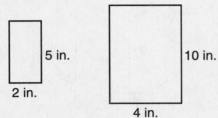

5 in.

10 in.

2 in.

4 in.

2.

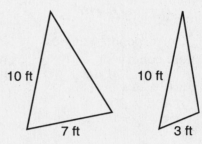

10 ft

10 ft

7 ft

3 ft

3.

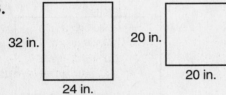

32 in.

20 in.

24 in.

20 in.

4.

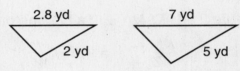

2.8 yd

7 yd

2 yd

5 yd

Find the value of x in each pair of similar polygons.

5.

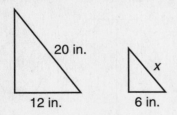

20 in.

x

12 in.

6 in.

6.

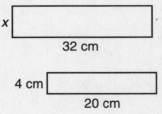

x

32 cm

4 cm

20 cm

7.

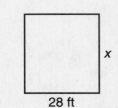

15 ft

12 ft

x

28 ft

8.

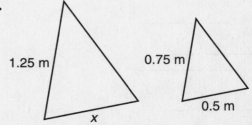

1.25 m

0.75 m

x

0.5 m

9-4 Study Guide

Triangles and Quadrilaterals

Triangles may be classified by the measures of their angles.

Classification by Angle	
Acute	all angles acute
Right	one right angle
Obtuse	one obtuse angle

Classification by Sides	
Scalene	all sides different lengths
Isosceles	two sides the same length
Equilateral	three sides the same length

Sides and angles are also used to classify quadrilaterals.

  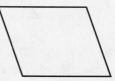

trapezoid,
only one pair
of parallel
sides

parallelogram,
both pairs of
opposite sides
parallel

rectangle,
a parallelogram
with four right
angles

rhombus,
a parallelogram
with four sides
the same length

square,
a parallelogram
with four right
angles and four
sides the same length

Classify each triangle by its sides and by its angles.

  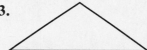 

1.
2.
3.
4.

Name every quadrilateral that describes each figure. Then underline the name that best describes the figure.

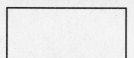  

5.
6.
7.
8.

*Mathematics: Applications
and Connections, Course 2*

9-4 Practice

Triangles and Quadrilaterals

Classify each triangle by its sides and by its angles.

1.

2.

3.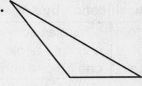

4.

5.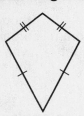

6.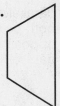

Name every quadrilateral that describes each figure. Then state which name best describes the figure.

7.

8.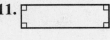

9.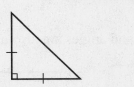

10.

11.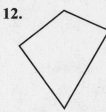

12.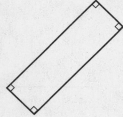

13.

14.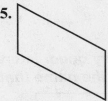

15.

16. Which quadrilaterals have four congruent sides?

17. A figure is a rectangle but not a rhombus. Draw the figure.

9-5 Study Guide

Tessellations

A **tessellation,** or tiling, is an arrangement of polygons that completely covers a plane surface without leaving gaps or overlapping.

The sum of the angle measures at any vertex of a tessellation is 360°. To determine whether a regular polygon tessellates, divide 360 by the measure of any angle of the polygon. If the quotient is a whole number, the polygon tessellates.

Examples   **1**   **hexagon**
The measure of an angle is 120°. 360 ÷ 120 = 3. A hexagon can be used to form a tessellation.

2   **pentagon**
The measure of an angle is 108°. 360 ÷ 108 = 3.$\overline{3}$. A pentagon cannot be used to form a tessellation.

To determine how a combination of regular polygons tessellates, find a way that the sum of the angles at each vertex equals 360°. There may be more than one way.

Example 3   **If an equilateral triangle, a square, and a regular hexagon are used in a tessellation, how many of each do you need at a vertex?**

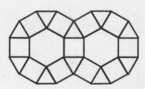

Each angle of an equilateral triangle measures 60°.
Each angle of a square measures 90°.
Each angle of a regular hexagon measures 120°. Try one of each: 60 + 90 + 120 = 270. That is not enough.
Try 1 triangle, 2 squares and 1 hexagon:
60 + 90 + 90 + 120 = 360.
One possibility is 1 triangle, 2 squares, and 1 hexagon.

Assume that each polygon is regular. Determine whether it can be used by itself to make a tessellation.

1. triangle   **2.** octagon   **3.** heptagon

The following regular polygons tessellate. Determine how many of each polygon you need at each vertex. Then sketch the tessellation.

4. dodecagon, triangle   **5.** triangle, square

Mathematics: Applications and Connections, Course 2

Practice

Tessellations

Determine whether each polygon can be used by itself to make a tessellation. Verify your results by finding the number of angles at a vertex. The sum of the measures of the angles of each polygon is given.

1. triangle; 180°

2. decagon; 1,440°

3. pentagon; 540°

4. heptagon; 900°

5. nonagon; 1,260°

6. quadrilateral; 360°

7. hexagon; 720°

8. dodecagon; 1,800°

9. octagon; 1,080°

10. Sketch a tessellation made with regular triangles and regular hexagons.

The following regular polygons tessellate. Determine how many of each polygon you need at each vertex. Then sketch the tessellation.

11. triangle, square

12. triangle, square, dodecagon

9-6 Study Guide

Translations

You can make changes in the polygons that tessellate to create new pattern units that will tessellate. One way to do this is by using a **translation,** or a slide.

Example 1 Change the square by sliding a piece from the left to the right to make a new pattern piece.

Then change all the squares in a tessellation the same way.

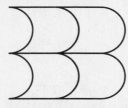

You can make more complex tessellations by doing two translations.

Example 2 Make two changes to create a pattern unit. Then complete the tessellation.

 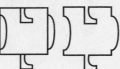 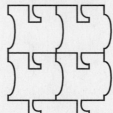

Complete the pattern unit for each translation. Then draw the tessellation.

1.

2.

3.

Mathematics: Applications and Connections, Course 2

9-6 Practice

Translations

Complete the pattern unit for each translation. Then draw the tessellation.

1.

2.

3.

4.

5.

6.

7. Can the puzzle piece at the right tessellate?

Mathematics: Applications and Connections, Course 2

9-7

Study Guide

Reflections

Figures that match exactly when folded in half have a **line of symmetry**.
Some figures have more than one line of symmetry.

Examples   one line of symmetry   more than one line   no line of symmetry
of symmetry

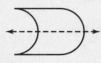   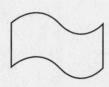

You can create figures that have a line of symmetry by using a **reflection**.
A reflection is a mirror image across a line of symmetry.

Example

You can make Escher-like drawings using reflections.

Example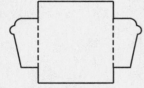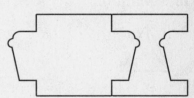

Draw all lines of symmetry.

1.

2.

3.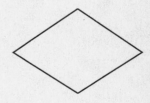

Complete both pattern units for each reflection. Then draw the tessellation.

4.

5.

6.

73   *Mathematics: Applications and Connections*, Course 2

9-7 **Practice**

Reflections

Draw all lines of symmetry.

1.

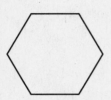

2.

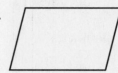

3.

4.

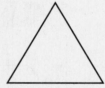

Complete both pattern units for each reflection. Then draw the tessellation.

5.

6.

7. Complete the tessellation described
   by the pattern shown below.

*Mathematics: Applications
and Connections, Course 2*

10-1 **Study Guide**

Squares and Square Roots

When you multiply a number by itself, you are finding the square of the number.

Examples

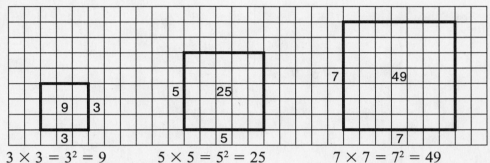

$3 \times 3 = 3^2 = 9$ $5 \times 5 = 5^2 = 25$ $7 \times 7 = 7^2 = 49$
The square of 3 is 9. The square of 5 is 25. The square of 7 is 49.

If $a^2 = b$, then a is the square root of b. The symbol, $\sqrt{}$ called a **radical sign,** is used to represent a nonnegative square root. Read $\sqrt{9}$ as "the square root of 9."

Examples Find $\sqrt{9}$. Find $\sqrt{16}$. Find $\sqrt{64}$.
Since $3^2 = 9$, Since $4^2 = 16$, Since $8^2 = 64$,
$\sqrt{9} = 3$. $\sqrt{16} = 4$. $\sqrt{64} = 8$.

Find the square of each number.

1. 9 **2.** 4 **3.** 10 **4.** 8

5. 24 **6.** 30 **7.** 15 **8.** 40

Find each square root.

9. 4 **10.** 64 **11.** 16 **12.** 121

13. 400 **14.** 2,500 **15.** 144 **16.** 169

17. 1 **18.** 36 **19.** 3,600 **20.** 100

10-1 Practice

Squares and Square Roots

Find the square of each number.

1. 4   2. 5   3. 8

4. 17   5. 9   6. 22

7. 40   8. 45   9. 31

Find each square root.

10. $\sqrt{169}$ 11. $\sqrt{900}$ 12. $\sqrt{81}$

13. $\sqrt{1,024}$ 14. $\sqrt{324}$ 15. $\sqrt{100}$

16. $\sqrt{361}$ 17. $\sqrt{1,225}$ 18. $\sqrt{2,500}$

19. $\sqrt{2,025}$ 20. $\sqrt{576}$ 21. $\sqrt{729}$

22. Find the length of the side of a square whose area is 1,156 in^2.

23. Find the area of a square whose side is 38 cm.

10-2 Study Guide

Estimating Square Roots

Estimate to find the square root of a number that is not a perfect square.

Example   **Estimate $\sqrt{95}$.**

$81 < 95 < 100$ Find the last perfect square less than 95 and the first perfect square greater than 95.

$\sqrt{81} < \sqrt{95} < \sqrt{100}$ Take the square root of each number. The square root of 95 is between the square root of 81 and the square root of 100.

$9 < \sqrt{95} < 10$ Find the square roots. The square root of 95 is between 9 and 10.

Since 95 is closer to 100 than to 81, $\sqrt{95}$ is closer to 10 than to 9.

The best whole number estimate for $\sqrt{95}$ is 10.

Estimate each square root to the nearest whole number.

1. $\sqrt{46}$ 2. $\sqrt{15}$ 3. $\sqrt{78}$ 4. $\sqrt{97}$

5. $\sqrt{10}$ 6. $\sqrt{50}$ 7. $\sqrt{62}$ 8. $\sqrt{33}$

Use a calculator to find each square root to the nearest tenth.

9. $\sqrt{150}$ 10. $\sqrt{391}$ 11. $\sqrt{84}$ 12. $\sqrt{5}$

13. $\sqrt{87}$ 14. $\sqrt{200}$ 15. $\sqrt{185}$ 16. $\sqrt{787}$

10-2 Practice

Estimating Square Roots

Estimate each square root to the nearest whole number.

1. $\sqrt{13}$

2. $\sqrt{27}$

3. $\sqrt{60}$

4. $\sqrt{84}$

5. $\sqrt{101}$

6. $\sqrt{72}$

7. $\sqrt{97}$

8. $\sqrt{47}$

9. $\sqrt{35}$

10. $\sqrt{58}$

11. $\sqrt{145}$

12. $\sqrt{10}$

Use a calculator to find each square root to the nearest tenth.

13. $\sqrt{800}$

14. $\sqrt{189}$

15. $\sqrt{850}$

16. $\sqrt{123}$

17. $\sqrt{50}$

18. $\sqrt{369}$

19. $\sqrt{450}$

20. $\sqrt{399}$

21. $\sqrt{150}$

22. $\sqrt{220}$

23. $\sqrt{1,200}$

24. $\sqrt{37}$

25. $\sqrt{1,869}$

26. $\sqrt{24}$

27. $\sqrt{296}$

10-3 Study Guide

The Pythagorean Theorem

The longest side of a right triangle is the **hypotenuse.** The hypotenuse is the side opposite the right angle. The other two sides of the triangle are the **legs.**

The **Pythagorean Theorem** relates the lengths of the sides of a right triangle.

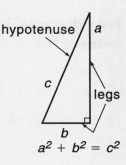

For any right triangle, the sum of the squares of the lengths of the legs (a and b) is equal to the square of the length of the hypotenuse (c).

You can use the Pythagorean Theorem to find the length of a side of a right triangle if the lengths of the other two sides are known.

Example   **Find the length of the leg.**

$$a^2 + b^2 = c^2$$
$$5^2 + b^2 = 10^2$$
$$25 + b^2 = 100$$
$$25 - 25 + b^2 = 100 - 25$$
$$b^2 = 75$$
$$b = \sqrt{75}$$
$$b \approx 8.660254038$$

The length of the leg (to the nearest tenth of an inch) is 8.7 in.

If the lengths of the sides of a right triangle can be substituted into the Pythagorean Theorem so that $a^2 + b^2 = c^2$, then the triangle is a right triangle.

Find the missing measure for each right triangle. Round to the nearest tenth.

1. a: 8 m; b: 15 m

2. a: 6 ft; b: 9 ft

3. a: 10 km; c: 26 km

4. b: 7 yd; c: 12 yd

5. a: 7 in.; b: 10 in.

6. a: 9 yd; b: 40 yd

7. a: 12 cm; c: 20 cm

8. b: 5 ft; c: 9 ft

Given the lengths of the sides of a triangle, determine whether each triangle is a right triangle. Write yes or no.

9. 20 in., 21 in., 29 in.

10. 8 ft, 11 ft, 13 ft

11. 7 yd, 24 yd, 25 yd

12. 7 cm, 9 cm, 12 cm

Mathematics: Applications and Connections, Course 2

10-3 Practice

The Pythagorean Theorem

Find the missing measure for each right triangle. Round to the nearest tenth.

1. *a*: 8 yd; *b*: 10 yd

2. *b*: 6 yd; *c*: 14 yd

3. *a*: 30 ft; *c*: 50 ft

4. *a*: 12 mm; *b*: 8 mm

5. *a*: 5 cm; *b*: 13 cm

6. *a*: 17 m; *b*: 25 m

Write an equation to solve for x. Then solve. Round to the nearest tenth.

7.
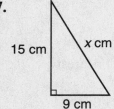
15 cm   *x* cm
9 cm

8.
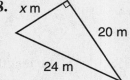
x m   20 m
24 m

9.
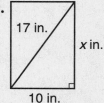
17 in.   *x* in.
10 in.

10.
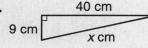
40 cm
9 cm   *x* cm

11.
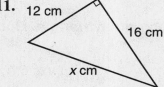
12 cm   16 cm
x cm

12.
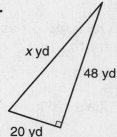
x yd   48 yd
20 yd

Given the lengths of the sides of a triangle, determine whether each triangle is a right triangle. Write yes or no.

13. 6 ft, 8 ft, 9 ft

14. 24 m, 32 m, 40 m

15. 9 cm, 39 cm, 41 cm

10-4 Study Guide

Area of Irregular Figures

One way to estimate the area of an irregular figure is to find the mean of the inner measure and the outer measure of the figure. The inner measure is the number of whole squares within the figure. The outer measure is the number of squares touching the figure anywhere plus the number of whole squares within the figure.

Example **Estimate the area of the irregular figure.**

inner measure (marked with dots):
68 units^2

outer measure (shaded squares):
110 units^2

mean: $\frac{68 + 110}{2} = 89$ units^2

An estimate of the area of the irregular figure is 89 units^2.

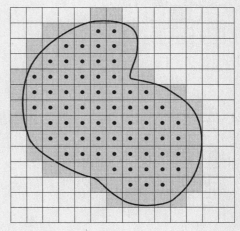

Estimate the area of each figure.

1.

2.

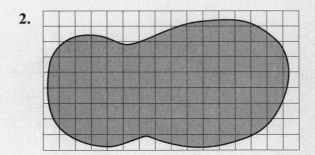

3.

4.

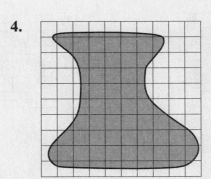

Mathematics: Applications and Connections, Course 2

10-4 Practice

Area of Irregular Figures

Estimate the area of each figure.

1.
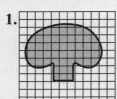

2.
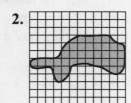

3.
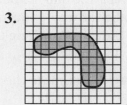

4.
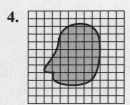

5.
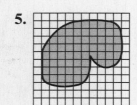

6.
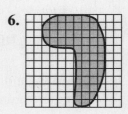

7.
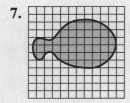

8.
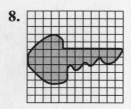

9.
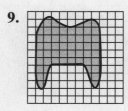

10.
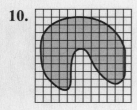

11.
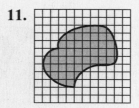

12.
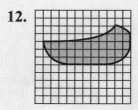

13. Draw the outline of a comb on a piece of centimeter grid paper. Estimate its area.

Mathematics: Applications and Connections, Course 2

10-5 Study Guide

Area of Triangles and Trapezoids

A triangle is a polygon that has three sides. The area of a triangle is equal to one-half the product of its base and height.

$$A = \frac{1}{2}bh$$

Example 1 **Find the area of the triangle.**

$A = \frac{1}{2}bh$

$A = \frac{1}{2} \times 12 \times 5$

$A = 6 \times 5$

$A = 30$ The area of the triangle is 30 m².

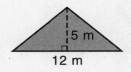
5 m
12 m

A **trapezoid** is a quadrilateral with exactly one pair of parallel sides. The area of a trapezoid is equal to one-half the product of its height times the sum of its bases.

$$A = \frac{1}{2}h(a + b)$$

Example 2 **Find the area of the trapezoid.**

$A = \frac{1}{2}h(a + b)$

$A = \frac{1}{2}(8)(15 + 12)$

$A = \frac{1}{2}(8)(27)$

$A = 4(27)$

$A = 108$ The area of the trapezoid is 108 cm².

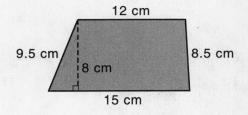
12 cm
9.5 cm
8.5 cm
8 cm
15 cm

Find the area of each triangle to the nearest tenth.

1. base: 10 in.
height: 20 in.

2. base: 4 m
height: 9 m

3. base: 15 cm
height: 12 cm

4. base: 2.4 cm
height: 10 cm

5. base: 2.8 m
height: 1.2 m

6. base: $2\frac{1}{2}$ ft
height: 6 ft

Find the area of each trapezoid to the nearest tenth.

7. bases: 6 m, 9 m
height: 4 m

8. bases: 10 ft, 15 ft
height: 20 ft

9. bases: 7.6 cm, 10 cm
height: 8 cm

Mathematics: Applications and Connections, Course 2

10-5 Practice

Area of Triangles and Trapezoids

Find the area of each triangle.

1.
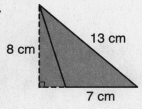
8 cm
13 cm
7 cm

2.
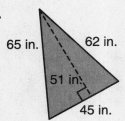
65 in.   62 in.
51 in.
45 in.

3. base: 12 ft
height: 7 ft

4. base: 17 m
height: 6 m

5. base: 5 km
height: 13 km

6. base: $3\frac{1}{2}$ in.
height: $1\frac{5}{8}$ in.

7. base: 3.9 mm
height: 7.2 mm

8. base: 10 yd
height: 20 yd

9. base: 7 km
height: 4.2 km

Find the area of each trapezoid.

10.
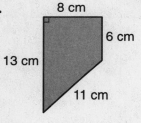
8 cm
6 cm
13 cm
11 cm

11.
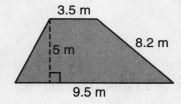
3.5 m
5 m   8.2 m
9.5 m

12. bases: 6 ft, 10 ft
height: 3 ft

13. bases: 10 in., 13 in.
height: 7.5 in.

14. bases: 8.4 m, 9.1 m
height: 12.8 m

15. bases: $4\frac{1}{3}$ ft, $2\frac{1}{4}$ ft
height: 6 ft

16. bases: 12 yd, 7 yd
height: 15 yd

17. bases: 35 in., 15 in.
height: 30 in.

18. bases: 7.1 m, 3.2 m
height: 6.8 m

10-6 Study Guide

Area of Circles

The area of a circle is equal to pi (π) times the square of the radius of the circle.

$$A = \pi r^2$$

Example 1 **Find the area of the circle.**

First find the radius.

$r = \frac{1}{2} \times 250$ The radius is $\frac{1}{2}$ of the diameter.

$r = 125$

Then find the area.
$A = \pi r^2$
$A \approx 3.14 \times 125^2$
$A \approx 3.14 \times 15{,}625$ *Replace π with 3.14 and r with 125.*
$A \approx 49{,}062.5$ The area of the circle is about 49,062.5 cm².

 250 cm

You can use the formula for the area of a circle to find the radius when the area is known.

Example 2 **Find the radius of a circle if its area is 452 ft².**

$A = \pi r^2$
$452 \approx 3.14 \times r^2$ *Replace A with 452 and π with 3.14.*
$452 \div 3.14 \approx (3.14 \times r^2) \div 3.14$ *Divide each side by 3.14.*
$143.9 \approx r^2$
$\sqrt{143.9} \approx r$
$12 \approx r$ The radius of the circle is about 12 ft.

Find the area of each circle to the nearest tenth.

1. 4 m

2. 20 km

3. 9 in.

4. 14 cm

5. radius 8 cm

6. diameter 10 ft

7. radius 4.5 m

8. diameter 24 ft

Find the length of the radius of each circle given the following areas. Round answers to the nearest tenth.

9. 314 cm²

10. 113 ft²

11. 707 m²

12. 1,256 in²

Mathematics: Applications and Connections, Course 2

10-6 Practice

Area of Circles

Find the area of each circle to the nearest tenth. Use 3.14 for π.

1.
6 m

2.
22 in.

3.
23 ft

4.
8 in.

5.
14 m

6.
3.5 cm

7.
16 ft

8.
3 cm

9.
15 km

10. diameter 9 km

11. radius 24 ft

12. radius 1 m

Find the radius of each circle given the following areas. Round to the nearest tenth.

13. 15 cm^2

14. 100 m^2

15. 200 ft^2

16. 12.4 in^2

17. 2.25 km^2

18. 102.48 m^2

Mathematics: Applications and Connections, Course 2

10-7 Study Guide

Integration: Probability
Area Models

Determine the probability that a randomly-dropped
counter will fall in the shaded area. Each small square
has an area of 1 ft^2.

The area of the entire region is 100 ft^2.
The area of the shaded region is about 40 ft^2.

$$\text{probability} = \frac{\text{number of ways an event can occur}}{\text{number of possible outcomes}}$$

$$= \frac{40}{100} \text{ or } \frac{2}{5}$$

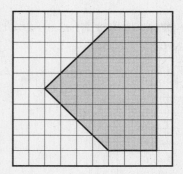

**Find the probability that a randomly-dropped counter
will fall in the shaded region.**

1.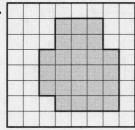

2.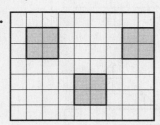

3.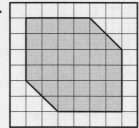

4.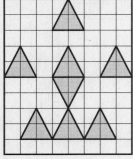

5.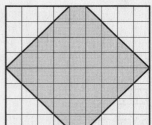

6.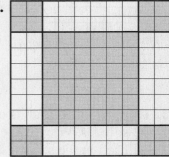

*Mathematics: Applications
and Connections*, Course 2

10-7 Practice

Integration: Probability
Area Models

**Find the probability that a randomly-dropped counter will fall
in the shaded region.**

1.

2.

3.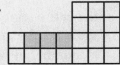

4.

5.

6.

7.

8.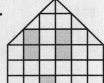

9.

10.

11.

12.

13. Draw a square 4 units on a side on a piece of grid paper. Shade in
12 squares. What is the probability that a randomly-dropped counter
will fall in the shaded area?

14. Draw a square 6 units on a side of a piece of grid paper. Shade in
14 squares. What is the probability that a randomly-dropped counter
will fall in the shaded area?

11-1 Study Guide

Percent and Estimation

You can use these two methods to estimate with percents.

Example 1 **Estimate 77% of 800. Use a fraction.**

77% is about 75%, which is $\frac{3}{4}$.

$\frac{3}{4}$ of $800 = \frac{3}{4} \times 800$ or 600

So, 77% of 800 is about 600.

Example 2 **Estimate 0.5% of 692. Find 1% and multiply.**

0.5% is half of 1%.   *692 rounds to 700.*

Recall that 1% means $\frac{1}{100}$.

$\frac{1}{100} \times 700 = 7$

$\frac{1}{2}$ of 7 is 3.5. So, 0.5% of 692 is about 3.5.

Example 3 **Estimate 122% of 42. Use the meaning of percent method.**

122% is about 120%.   *120% = 100% + 20%*

$42(100\% + 20\%) = 42(100\%) + 42(20\%)$ *20% means $2 \times 10\%$.*

$\qquad\qquad\qquad = 42 + 8.4$

$\qquad\qquad\qquad = 50.4$ So, 122% of 42 is about 50.4.

Write the fraction, decimal, mixed number, or whole number equivalent of each percent that could be used to estimate.

1. 24%   2. 35%   3. 500%   4. 0.9%

5. 37.2%   6. $\frac{12}{13}$%   7. 250%   8. 48.8%

Estimate.

9. 11% of 67   10. 50% of 78   11. 1% of 54

12. 150% of 179   13. 67% of 450   14. 79% of 590

15. 0.4% of 200   16. 300% of 61   17. 52% of 218

Practice

Percent and Estimation

Estimate the percent shaded. Then count to find the exact percent.

1.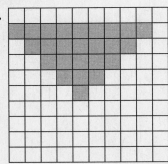

2.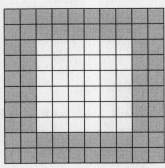

3.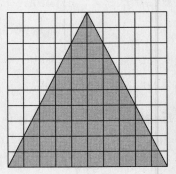

Write the fraction, decimal, mixed number, or whole number equivalent of each percent that could be used to estimate.

4. 42%

5. 77%

6. 9.2%

7. 312%

8. 450%

9. $\frac{8}{9}$%

10. $24\frac{1}{3}$%

11. 0.1%

12. 500%

Estimate.

13. 51% of 128

14. 310% of 500

15. 76% of 200

16. 0.49% of 10

17. 12% of $98\frac{1}{2}$

18. 32.9% of 90

19. 89% of 300

20. 153% of 20

21. 0.9% of 250

22. 19% of 450

23. 1% of 98

24. 24% of 8

Mathematics: Applications and Connections, Course 2

11-2 Study Guide

Integration: Algebra
The Percent Equation

In the percent proportion, $\frac{r}{100}$ is the rate. Let $R = \frac{r}{100}$.

Then $\frac{P}{B} = \frac{r}{100}$ becomes $\frac{P}{B} = R$.

Rewrite the equation at the right above to make it easier to solve equations when the rate and base are given.

$$P = R \cdot B$$

Examples **1** **What number is 35% of 480?**

$P = R \cdot B$ *Replace R with 0.35 and B with 480.*
$P = 0.35 \cdot 480$
$P = 168$
So, 35% of 480 is 168.

    2 **56 is what percent of 224?**

$P = R \cdot B$ *Replace P with 56 and B with 224.*
$56 = 224R$

$\frac{56}{224} = \frac{224R}{224}$

$0.25 = R$

So, 56 is 25% of 224.

Write an equation for each problem. Then solve.

1. 63 is what percent of 42?

2. 35% of what number is 49?

3. Find 12% of 225.

4. 198 is 60% of what number?

5. What percent of 360 is 108?

6. 792 is 90% of what number?

7. 85% of 460 is what number?

8. 6% of what number is 9?

9. 95 is what percent of 50?

10. What is 29% of $17?

11-2 Practice

Integration: Algebra
The Percent Equation

Write an equation for each problem. Then solve. Round answers to the nearest tenth.

1. 18 is 24% of what number?

2. 25% of 176 is what number?

3. 45% of what number is 121.5?

4. 80% of what number is 94?

5. 32.5% of 256 is what number?

6. What percent of 125 is 25?

7. $18\frac{3}{4}$ is 25% of what number?

8. 15% of 290 is what number?

9. What percent of 224 is 28?

10. 344.8 is what percent of 862?

11. What number is 60% of 605?

12. 32% of 250 is what number?

11-3 Study Guide

Integration: Statistics
Making Circle Graphs

A **circle graph** shows how a whole is divided into parts.

Ocean	Pacific	Atlantic	Indian	Arctic
Area (in millions of mi²)	64.2	33.4	28.4	5.1

To make a circle graph for the data in the table, first find the total area of the oceans: $64.2 + 33.4 + 28.4 + 5.1 = 131.1$.

Then find the ratio that compares the area of each of the oceans to the total area. Use a calculator. Round to the nearest hundredth.

Ocean Areas

Pacific: $\frac{64.2}{131.1} = 0.49$ Indian: $\frac{28.4}{131.1} = 0.22$

Atlantic: $\frac{33.4}{131.1} = 0.25$ Arctic: $\frac{5.1}{131.1} = 0.04$

To find the number of degrees for each section of the graph, multiply each ratio by 360°. Round to the nearest degree.

Pacific: $0.49 \times 360° = 176°$ Indian: $0.22 \times 360° = 79°$
Atlantic: $0.25 \times 360° = 90°$ Arctic: $0.04 \times 360° = 14°$

Use a compass and protractor to construct a circle and angles whose measures are 17°, 90°, 79°, and 14°. Note that the sum of the degrees is not 360° due to rounding.

Make a circle graph to show the data in the chart.

Continent	Area (in millions of mi²)
Europe	3.8
Asia	17.4
North America	9.4
South America	6.9
Africa	11.7
Oceania	3.3
Antarctica	5.4

11-3 Practice

Integration: Statistics
Making Circle Graphs

Write a ratio that compares the number of students enrolled in each category of school to the total number of students in school.

1990 School Enrollment by Grade (millions)	
Grades K-8	33.6
Grades 9-12	12.2
College	13.2
Total	59.0

1. grades K-8

2. grades 9-12

3. college

Use the ratios from Exercises 1–3 to find the number of degrees in each category that would be on a circle graph. Round degree measures to the nearest whole number.

4. grades K-8   5. grades 9-12   6. college

7. Make a circle graph that shows the composition of the school population in 1990.

**1990
School Enrollment (millions)**

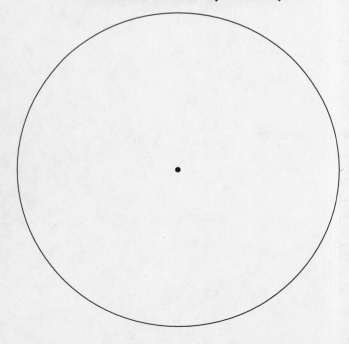

11-4 Study Guide

Integration: Statistics
Using Statistics to Predict

Data gathered by surveying a random sample of the population may be used to make predictions about the entire population.

Example   **200 people from a town of 28,000 people were chosen at random and asked if they thought the town needed more bicycle paths. 78 out of the 200 people responded Yes. 84 responded No. Of those surveyed, 38 were undecided. Predict how many of the 28,000 people in the town think more bicycle paths are needed.**

78 out of 200 is 39%.
39% of 28,000 = 0.39 × 28,000 or 10,920

You can predict that about 10,920 people think more bicycle paths are needed.

Members of a seventh-grade class were surveyed to find out how much they would be willing to pay to go on a class trip. The results are shown in the chart.

Price Range	$10 – $20	$21 – $30	$31 – $40	$41 – $50
Students	4	12	20	14

1. What was the sample size?

2. What percent of the students said they would pay $31 to $40?

3. What percent of the students would go on the trip if it cost $30?

4. If there are 360 students in the seventh-grade class, about how many would go on the trip if it cost $30?

Predict each outcome.

5. In a poll of 100 people, 55 said they would vote for Alvarez for city council. If 24,000 people vote in the election, about how many will vote for Alvarez?

6. A survey showed that 129 out of 300 people in a factory bought lunch in the cafeteria. If the factory employs 2,900 people, about how many buy lunch in the cafeteria?

Name_____ Date_____

Integration: Statistics
Using Statistics to Predict

Of the TV households surveyed by the
Nielson Media Research Company, the top
sports shows of 1990-1991 are listed in the
table at the right.

Top Sports Shows, 1990-91	
Show	% of TV households
1. Super Bowl XXV	41.9
2. NFC Championship	28.5
3. AFC Playoff Bengals vs. Raiders	24.7
4. NFC Playoff Saints vs. Bears	24.2

1. How many households in a town with
   40,000 households might you expect to
   have watched Super Bowl XXV?

2. How many households in a town with 80,000 households might you
   expect to have watched the fourth top show?

3. How many households in a town with 100,000 households might you
   expect to have watched a program *other* than the NFC Championship
   game?

Mrs. Romano surveyed her 7th-grade class about
their favorite foods. The results are shown in the
table at the right.

Favorite Food	Number of Students
spaghetti	10
pizza	9
hamburgers	4
tacos	4
fried chicken	3

4. What was the sample size?

5. What percent of students liked
   pizza best?

6. Mr. Peters' class has 24 students in it but otherwise is about the same as
   Mrs. Romano's class. How many students would you expect to like
   spaghetti the best?

7. How many students in Mr. Peters' class would you expect to not like
   tacos the best?

8. For the entire 7th-grade class of 250 students, how many would you
   expect to like fried chicken the best?

11-5 Study Guide

Percent of Change

To find the percent of change, first find the amount of increase or decrease. Then find the ratio of that amount to the original amount and express the ratio as a percent.

Examples **1** **Last year, 2,376 people attended the rodeo. This year, attendance was 2,954. What was the percent of increase in rodeo attendance?**

$2,954 - 2,376 = 578$ *Find the amount of the increase.*

$\frac{578}{2,376} \approx 0.24$ *Compare the amount of increase to the original amount.*

Rodeo attendance increased by about 24%.

2 **John's grade on the first math exam was 94. His grade on the second math exam was 86. What was the percent of decrease in John's grade?**

$94 - 86 = 8$ *Find the amount of decrease.*

$\frac{8}{94} \approx 0.09$ *Compare the amount of decrease to the original amount.*

John's math grade decreased by about 9%.

Find the percent of change. Round to the nearest whole percent.

1. old: $12
new: $15

2. old: $40
new: $18

3. old: 100
new: 67

4. old: $90
new: $135

5. old: $144
new: $108

6. old: 6.5
new: 8

7. old: 280
new: 200

8. old: $86
new: $70

9. old: 69
new: 100

10. old: 20.8
new: 12.2

11. old: 45
new: 15

12. old: $75
new: $15

11-5 Practice

Percent of Change

Find the percent of change. Round to the nearest whole percent.

1. old: $8
new: $12

2. old: $45
new: $30

3. old: $0.39
new: $0.26

4. old: $75
new: $60

5. old: $350
new: $400

6. old: 0.32
new: 0.48

7. old: 35
new: 70

8. old: 6.8
new: 8.2

9. old: 1.5
new: 2.5

10. old: $84
new: $100

11. old: $250
new: $100

12. old: $87.05
new: $100

16. old: $12.50
new: $15

17. old: $30
new: $110

18. old: 16.5
new: 20

11-6 Study Guide

Discount and Sales Tax

Sales tax is a percent of the purchase price.

Example 1   **Find the total price of a $17.75 soccer ball if the sales tax is 6%.**

Method 1

Find the amount of tax.
  6% of $17.75 = t
  $0.06 \times \$17.75 = 1.07$
The sales tax is $1.07.

Add to find the total cost.
$17.75 + \$1.07 = \$18.82$

Method 2

Add the percent of tax to 100%.
$100\% + 6\% = 106\%$
The total price will be 106% of the price of the soccer ball.

Multiply to find the total cost.
$\$17.75 \times 1.06 = \$18.82$

The total cost of the soccer ball is $18.82.

Discount is the amount the sales price is reduced.

Example 2   **Find the price of a $69.50 tennis racket that is on sale for 20% off.**

$69.50 \times 20\%$
$\$69.50 \times 0.20 = \$13.90$
$\$69.50 - \$13.90 = \$55.60$

Find 20% of $69.50.
The discount is $13.90.
Subtract to find the sale price.

The tennis racket will cost $55.60 on sale.

Find the sales tax or discount to the nearest cent.

1. $22.95 jeans, 7% tax

2. $39.00 sweater, 25% off

3. $35 necklace, 40% off

4. $115.48 watch, 6% tax

Find the total cost or sale price to the nearest cent.

5. $16.99 book, 5% tax

6. $13.99 calendar, 50% off

7. $129.40 rocking horse, 15% off

8. $349 television, 6% tax

$B=(1+r)^t$

11-6 Practice

Discount and Sales Tax

Find the sales tax or discount to the nearest cent.

1. $34 shoes; 6% tax

2. $32.50 watch; 25% discount

3. $12.98 compact disc, 7% tax

4. $18.00 radio; 15% discount

5. $46.95 coat, 30% off

6. $1.99 socks; 5.5% tax

Find the total cost or sale price to the nearest cent.

7. $149.95 disc player, 20% off

8. $12.99 T-shirt; 6% tax

9. $24.95 video movie, 10% off

10. $8.99 toy, $6\frac{1}{2}$% tax

11. $59.00 power tool, 5% tax

12. $8.95 cassette, 15% off

Find the rate of discount to the nearest percent.

13. regular price, $30
    sale price, $20

14. regular price, $198
    sale price, $169

15. regular price, $18.95
    sale price, $16.00

16. regular price, $48
    sale price, $34

17. regular price, $80
    sale price, $62.95

18. regular price, $75
    sale price, $70

Mathematics: Applications and Connections, Course 2

11-7 Study Guide

Simple Interest

Simple interest (I) is calculated by multiplying the principal (p), times the rate (r), which is given as a percent, times the time (t) given in years: $I = prt$.

Example   **Find the interest earned on $1,250 at 6.5% for 9 months.**

$I = prt$

$p = \$1,250$, $r = 6.5\%$, or 0.065, and $t = \frac{9}{12}$ year, or 0.75 year.

$I = 1,250 \times 0.065 \times 0.75$
$I = 60.94$

The interest earned in 9 months is $60.94.

Find the interest to the nearest cent for each principal, interest rate, and time.

1. $500, 8%, 4 years

2. $1,600, 18%, 2 years

3. $480, 15%, 1.5 years

4. $725, 6%, 1.25 years

5. $2,890, 10%, 6 months

6. $668, 7.5%, 8 years

7. $903, 8.75%, 18 months

8. $4,275, 19%, 3 months

9. $210, 1%, 0.25 years

10. $100, 10%, 10 years

11-7 Practice

Simple Interest

Find the interest to the nearest cent for each principal, interest rate, and time.

1. $300, 5%, 3 years

2. $450.90, 10%, 1.8 years

3. $198, 14%, 6 months

4. $3,980, $6\frac{1}{2}$%, 4 years

5. $695, 11%, 1 year

6. $189.50, 8%, 2 years

7. $2,178, 12%, 5 years

8. $568, 16%, 8 months

Find the interest to the nearest cent on credit cards for each credit card balance, interest rate, and time.

9. $429, 18.5%, 1 year

10. $1,400, 16.5%, 8 months

11. $1,000, $22\frac{1}{2}$%, 6 months

12. $989, 17%, 2 years

13. $3,126, 19%, 9 months

14. $549, 21%, 2 years

15. $1,050, 16%, 2.5 years

16. $450, 22%, 1 year

Study Guide

Drawing Three-Dimensional Figures

Two-dimensional drawings of some common three-dimensional figures are
shown below.

rectangular prism   triangular prism   pyramid   cone   cylinder

If you know how a three-dimensional figure looks from different views,
you can make a two-dimensional drawing of the figure.

Example

two-dimensional drawing
of a three-dimensional figure

top   side   front

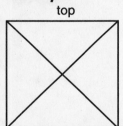 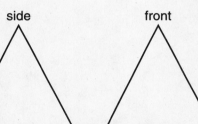 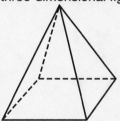

Draw a top, a side, and a front view of each figure.

1. 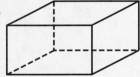   **2.** 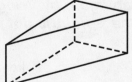   **3.**

Draw each three-dimensional figure given the different views of it.

4.   top   side   front

5. 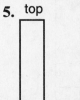 top   side   front

88   *Mathematics: Applications and Connections, Course 2*

Name _____ Date _____

12-1 Practice

Drawing Three-Dimensional Figures

Draw a top, a side, and a front view of each figure.

1. 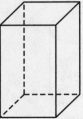   top   side   front

2.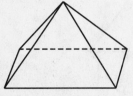

3.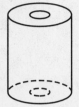

Make a perspective drawing of each figure by using the top, side, and front views, as shown. Use isometric dot paper if necessary.

4.   top   side   front

5.

12-2 **Study Guide**

Volume of Rectangular Prisms

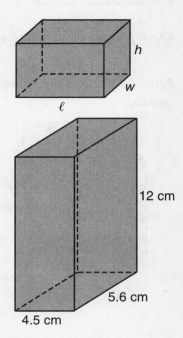

Volume is the measure of the space occupied by a solid figure. Volume is measured in cubic units.

The volume V of a rectangular prism is found by multiplying the length (ℓ), the width (w), and the height (h): $V = \ell wh$.

Example **Find the volume of the rectangular prism.**

$\ell = 5.6$ cm, $w = 4.5$ cm, and $h = 12$ cm

$V = \ell wh$
  $= 5.6 \times 4.5 \times 12$
  $= 302.4$

The volume of the rectangular prism is 302.4 cm³.

Find the volume of each rectangular prism to the nearest tenth.

1.

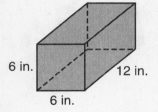

6 in. 12 in. 6 in.

2.

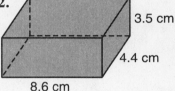

3.5 cm 4.4 cm 8.6 cm

3.

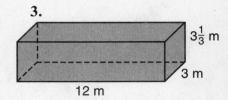

$3\frac{1}{3}$ m 3 m 12 m

4.

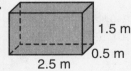

1.5 m 0.5 m 2.5 m

5.

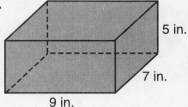

5 in. 7 in. 9 in.

6.

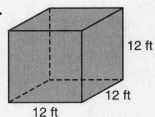

12 ft 12 ft 12 ft

7. length, 8 mm
width, 4 mm
height, 6 mm

8. length, 14 cm
width, 12 cm
height, 10 cm

9. length, 6.2 m
width, 5.5 m
height, 7 m

Mathematics: Applications and Connections, Course 2

12-2 Practice

Volume of Rectangular Prisms

Find the volume of each rectangular prism to the nearest tenth.

1.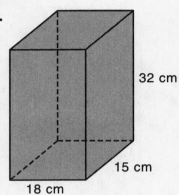

32 cm

15 cm

18 cm

2.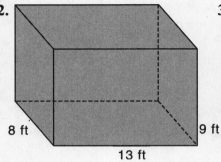

8 ft   9 ft

13 ft

3.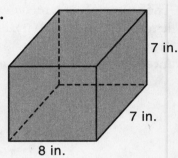

7 in.

7 in.

8 in.

4.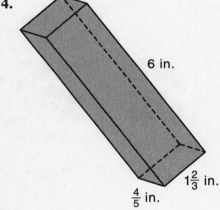

6 in.

$1\frac{2}{3}$ in.

$\frac{4}{5}$ in.

5.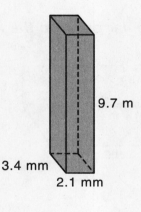

9.7 m

3.4 mm

2.1 mm

6.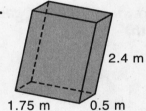

2.4 m

1.75 m   0.5 m

7. length, 8 mm
   width, 12 mm
   height, 10 mm

8. length, 7.5 cm
   width, 6.2 cm
   height, 8.1 cm

9. length, 9 ft
   width, 7 ft
   height, 12.5 ft

10. length, 7.6 in.
    width, 8.4 in.
    height, 15 in.

11. length, 16 cm
    width, 16 cm
    height, 12 cm

12. length, 18.3 cm
    width, 27 cm
    height, 21 cm

13. A cube has sides that are 9.2 inches long. What is the volume of the cube?

Mathematics: Applications and Connections, Course 2

12-3 Study Guide

Volume of Cylinders

The volume V of a cylinder is found by multiplying the area of the base (πr^2) times the height (h): $V = \pi r^2 h$.

Example   **Find the volume of the cylinder to the nearest tenth.**

$r = 6.3$ in. and $h = 20$ in.

$V = \pi r^2 h$
   $= 3.14 \times (6.3)^2 \times 20$
   $= 3.14 \times 39.69 \times 20$
   $= 2{,}492.532$

The volume of the cylinder is about 2,492.5 in^3.

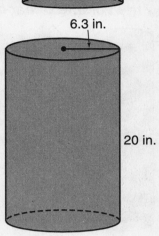

Find the volume of each cylinder to the nearest tenth.

1.   8 ft
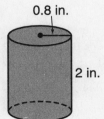
16 ft

2.   5 m
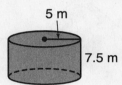
7.5 m

3.   20 cm
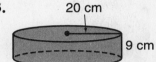
9 cm

4.   0.8 in.
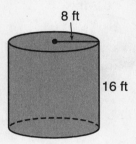
2 in.

5.   4 ft
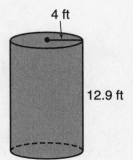
12.9 ft

6.   10 mm
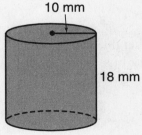
18 mm

7. radius, 7 cm
    height, 21 cm

8. radius, 3 cm
    height, 10 cm

9. radius, 5 inches
    height, 15 inches

           Mathematics: Applications and Connections, Course 2

12-3 Practice

Volume of Cylinders

Find the volume of each cylinder to the nearest tenth.

1.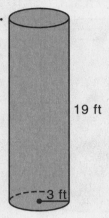
19 ft
3 ft

2.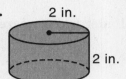
2 in.
2 in.

3.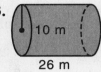
10 m
26 m

4.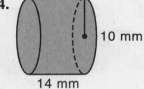
10 mm
14 mm

5.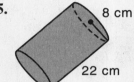
8 cm
22 cm

6.
20.5 in.
38.6 in.

7. height, 7 cm
   radius, 11 cm

8. height, 7.2 ft
   radius, 9.5 ft

9. height, 2 ft
   radius, 2 ft

10. height, 19 mm
    radius, 22 mm

11. height, 16 in.
    radius, 14 in.

12. height, $2\frac{1}{7}$ in.
    radius, 7 in.

13. A coffee can is 6.5 inches high and has a diameter of 5 inches. Find the volume of the can. Round to the nearest tenth.

Mathematics: Applications and Connections, Course 2

Name _____ **Date** _____

Study Guide

Surface Area of Rectangular Prisms

The surface area of a rectangular prism equals the sum of the areas of the faces.

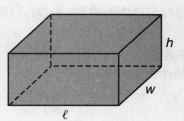

The surface area of a rectangular prism can be found by using the formula $A = 2\ell w + 2\ell h + 2wh$.

Example **Find the surface area of the rectangular prism.**

$\ell = 6.4$ cm, $w = 5.6$ cm, and $h = 4$ cm

$A = 2\ell w + 2\ell h + 2wh$
  $= 2(6.4)(5.6) + 2(6.4)(4) + 2(5.6)(4)$
  $= 71.68 + 51.2 + 44.8$
  $= 167.68$

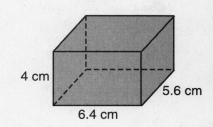

The surface area of the rectangular prism is 167.68 cm^2.

Find the surface area of each rectangular prism to the nearest tenth.

1.

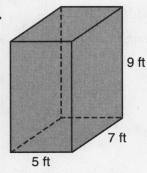

9 ft
7 ft
5 ft

2.

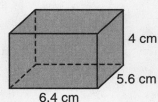

4 cm
5.6 cm
6.4 cm

3.

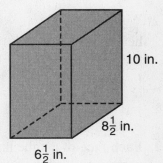

10 in.
$8\frac{1}{2}$ in.
$6\frac{1}{2}$ in.

4. length, 15 m
   width, 12 m
   height, 9 m

5. lencth, 9.6 cm
   width, 7.5 cm
   height, 7.7 cm

6. length, 100 in.
   width, 100 in.
   height, 50 in.

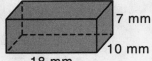 **Practice**

Surface Area of Rectangular Prisms

Find the surface area of each rectangular prism to the nearest tenth.

1.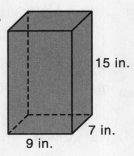
   7 mm
   10 mm
   18 mm

2.
   15 in.
   7 in.
   9 in.

3.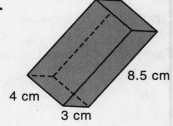
   8.5 cm
   4 cm
   3 cm

4. length, 2 m
   width, 6 m
   height, 9.5 m

5. length, 7 yd
   width, 2 yd
   height, 5 yd

6. length, $2\frac{1}{2}$ in.
   width, $1\frac{1}{4}$ in.
   height, 4 in.

7. length, 16.4 cm
   width, 12.3 cm
   height, 10.9 cm

8. length, $3\frac{1}{2}$ ft
   width, $1\frac{1}{3}$ ft
   height, $2\frac{1}{2}$ ft

9. length, 38 mm
   width, 32 mm
   height, 15 mm

10. Each face of a cube has an area of 12 square inches. What is the surface area of the cube?

11. A cube has a surface area of 108 square feet. What is the area of one face?

91

Mathematics: Applications and Connections, Course 2

12-5 Study Guide

Surface Area of Cylinders

To find the surface area of a cylinder, find the sum of the areas of the two circular bases and the area of the curved surface.

area of each circle $= \pi r^2$

area of both circles $= 2\pi r^2$

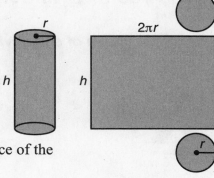

The length of the curved surface is equal to the circumference of the circle, so the area of the curved surface is $2\pi r \times h$.

The surface area of a cylinder is given by $2\pi r^2 + 2\pi rh$.

Example   **Find the surface area of the cylinder. Use 3.14 for π.**

$$A = 2\pi r^2 + 2\pi rh$$
$$= 2(3.14)(3^2) + 2(3.14)(3)(7)$$
$$= 56.52 + 131.88$$
$$= 188.4$$

The surface area of the cylinder is 188.4 ft^2.

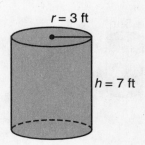

r = 3 ft
h = 7 ft

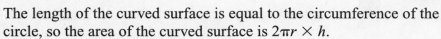

Find the surface area of each cylinder to the nearest tenth. Use 3.14 for π.

1.   10 mm

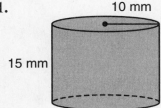

15 mm

2.   7.5 in.

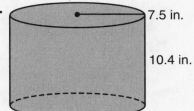

10.4 in.

3.   6 m

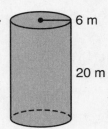

20 m

4. height, 14 m
    radius, 7 m

5. height, 70 ft
    radius, 10 ft

6. height, 6 cm
    radius, 21 cm

Mathematics: Applications and Connections, Course 2

12-5 Practice

Surface Area of Cylinders

Find the surface area of each cylinder to the nearest tenth. Use 3.14 for π.

1.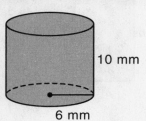
10 mm
6 mm

2. 3.5 ft
24 ft

3. 7 yd
4.8 yd

4. 8.5 in.
24.5 in.

5.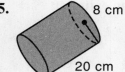
8 cm
20 cm

6. $2\frac{1}{2}$ ft
$4\frac{1}{3}$ ft

7. height, 12 cm
   radius, 9 cm

8. height, 3.2 ft
   radius, 4.5 ft

9. height, 7 mm
   radius, 8 mm

10. height, 18 ft
    radius, 20 ft

11. height, 6 in.
    radius, 9 in.

12. height, $10\frac{1}{2}$ yd
    radius, $9\frac{1}{4}$ yd

13. Find the surface area of a cylinder whose height is 18 inches and whose base has a diameter of 19 inches.

Study Guide

Theoretical and Experimental Probability

Theoretical probability is determined by finding the ratio of the number of ways an event can occur to the number of possible outcomes. **Experimental probability** is determined by conducting an experiment.

Example Julio tossed two coins and tallied the results. He repeated the experiment 20 times. Find the experimental and theoretical probabilities.

Outcome	Tally	Frequency
2 heads	ⅢⅢ I	6
1 head, 1 tail	ⅢⅢ ⅢⅢ I	11
2 tails	III	3

The experimental probability of tossing 1 head and 1 tail is $\frac{11}{20}$.

The possible outcomes for tossing two coins are: HH, HT, TH, TT. The theoretical probability of tossing 1 head and 1 tail is $\frac{2}{4}$, or $\frac{1}{2}$.

Perform the experiment described above 20 times. Record your results in the chart. Find the experimental probability for each outcome.

Outcome	Tally	Frequency
2 heads		
1 head, 1 tail		
2 tails		

One card is drawn from a 52-card deck. Find each theoretical probability.

1. P(heart)

2. P(king)

3. P(king, queen, or jack)

4. P(red)

5. P(red or black)

6. P(number less than 6)

Mathematics: Applications and Connections, Course 2

13-1 Practice

Theoretical and Experimental Probability

1. Find the theoretical probability of rolling an even number with a die.

2. Find the theoretical probability that a family of four children will be all girls.

3. Find the theoretical probability of choosing a winning three-digit number in the lottery.

4. Jessica tosses two coins four times. Twice both coins came up heads.

   a. What is the experimental probability of getting two heads?

   b. What is the theoretical probability of getting two heads?

   c. What is the theoretical probability of getting two tails?

   d. What is the theoretical probability of getting a head and a tail?

5. Suppose you have a child's play cube with one of the following letters on each face: A, B, C, D, E, or F. You toss the cube.

   a. What is the theoretical probability of turning up an A, B, or C?

   b. If you toss two identical cubes, what is the theoretical probability of turning up an A, A?

6. Suppose you have a bag containing two red marbles, two blue marbles, and two white marbles. You choose a marble without looking.

   a. What is the theoretical probability that you will choose a white or a blue marble?

   b. What is the theoretical probability that you will choose a red marble or a white marble?

Two dice are rolled. Find each theoretical probability.

7. a sum of 8   8. a sum less than 5   9. a sum of 12

13-2 Study Guide

Tree Diagrams

You can draw a tree diagram to find the number of possible combinations or outcomes.

Example **If you flip three coins, a nickel, a penny, and a quarter, how many different outcomes are possible?**

Nickel	Penny	Quarter	Outcomes
H	H	H	HHH
		T	HHT
	T	H	HTH
		T	HTT
T	H	H	THH
		T	THT
	T	H	TTH
		T	TTT

There are 8 possible outcomes.

Make a tree diagram and list the outcomes. Then give the total number of outcomes.

1. Spin each spinner.

2. Choose from red, blue, green, or yellow and large or small.

3. Choose soup or salad, fish or chicken, and ice cream or cake.

13-2 Practice

Tree Diagrams

For each situation, make a tree diagram to show all the outcomes in the sample space. Then give the total number of outcomes.

1. choosing chocolate or vanilla ice cream and choosing strawberry or apple pie

2. rolling a die and flipping a coin

3. choosing rolls, muffins, or fruit salad and choosing scrambled eggs, sliced ham, chicken or turkey casserole

4. choosing a red, blue, or white sweater and choosing a black, blue, or gray pair of slacks

13-3 Study Guide

The Counting Principle

The Counting Principle uses multiplication to find the number of possible outcomes.

> If event *M* can occur in *m* ways and is followed by event *N* that can occur in *n* ways, then the event *M* followed by *N* can occur in $m \times n$ ways.

Example   **Pinky's Pizza serves 11 different kinds of pizza with 3 choices of crust and in 4 different sizes. How many different selections are possible?**

Apply the Counting Principle.

number of kinds		*number of crusts*		*number of sizes*		*possible selections*
11	$\times$	3	$\times$	4	$=$	132

There are 132 possible pizza selections.

Use the Counting Principle to find the total number of outcomes in each situation.

1. The nursery has 14 different colored tulip bulbs. Each color comes in dwarf, average, or giant size. How many different kinds of bulbs are there?

2. The type of bicycle Elena wants comes in 12 different colors with 12 different colors of trim. There is also a choice of curved or straight handlebars. How many possible selections are there?

3. At a banquet, guests were given a choice of 4 entrees, 3 vegetables, soup or salad, 4 beverages, and 4 desserts. How many different selections were possible?

4. Ms. Nitobe is setting the combination lock on her briefcase. If she can choose any digit 0−9 for each of the 6 digits in the combination, how many possible combinations are there?

Mathematics: Applications and Connections, Course 2

13-3 Practice

The Counting Principle

Use the Counting Principle to find the total number of outcomes in each situation.

1. choosing a paint color from among 6 color choices, and choosing a wallpaper pattern from among 5 choices

2. flipping a penny, a nickel, and a dime

3. choosing the last three digits in a five-digit zip code if the first digit is 6, the second digit is 1, and no digit is used more than once

4. choosing one of three science courses, one of five mathematics courses, one of two English courses, and one of four social studies courses

5. choosing from one of three appetizers, one of four main dishes, one of six desserts, and one of four soft drinks

6. choosing a book with a mystery, science-fiction, romance, or adventure theme, choosing one of five different authors for each theme, and choosing paperback or hardcover for the type of book

7. choosing a phone number if the first three-digit combination can be one of 8 choices and if the last four digits can be any combination of digits from 1 to 9 without any repeated digits

13-4 Study Guide

Independent and Dependent Events

When the outcome of one event does not influence the outcome of a second event, the two events are **independent.** The probability of two independent events can be found by multiplying the probability of one event by the probability of the second event.

Example 1   If you draw a card from a deck numbered 1 through 8 and toss a die, what is the probability of getting a 4 and an even number?

$$P(4) = \tfrac{1}{8} \qquad P(\text{even}) = \tfrac{3}{6} \text{ or } \tfrac{1}{2}$$

$$P(4, \text{even}) = \tfrac{1}{8} \cdot \tfrac{1}{2} \text{ or } \tfrac{1}{16}$$

The probability of a 4 and an even number is $\tfrac{1}{16}$.

If the outcome of one event affects the outcome of a second event, the events are **dependent.**

Example 2   There are 6 black pens and 8 blue pens in a jar. If you take a pen without looking and then take another pen without replacing the first, what is the probability that you will get 2 black pens?

$$P(\text{black first}) = \tfrac{6}{14} \text{ or } \tfrac{3}{7}$$

$$P(\text{black second}) = \tfrac{5}{13} \quad \leftarrow \textit{There are 13 pens left; 5 are black.}$$

$$P(\text{black, black}) = \tfrac{3}{7} \cdot \tfrac{5}{13} \text{ or } \tfrac{15}{91}$$

The probability of choosing 2 black pens is $\tfrac{15}{91}$.

Tell whether each is independent or dependent.

1. selecting a sweater, selecting a shirt

2. choosing one card from a deck then choosing a second card without replacing the first

3. A wallet contains two $5 bills, two $10 bills, and three $20 bills. Two bills are selected without the first being replaced. Find $P(\$20, \$20)$.

4. Two dice are rolled. Find $P(6, \text{even})$.

Mathematics: Applications and Connections, Course 2

13-4 Practice

Independent and Dependent Events

Tell whether each event is independent or dependent. Explain.

1. rolling a die and then rolling a second die

2. choosing two cards from a deck so that they make a "pair" (the number value is the same)

3. selecting a compact disc from a storage case and then selecting a second disc without replacing the first

Find each probability.

4. Two dice are rolled. Find the probability that an even number is rolled on one die and an odd number is rolled on the second die.

5. Two coins are tossed in order. What is the probability of getting a head on the first coin and then getting a tail on the second coin?

6. Suppose you have a bag containing two red marbles, two blue marbles, and two white marbles. You choose two marbles without looking.

   a. What is the probability that you will choose a red marble and then a blue marble without replacing the red one?

   b. What is the probability that you will choose two red marbles in a row without replacing the first one?

7. A coin purse contains 10 pennies, 5 nickels, 3 dimes, and 2 quarters. Two coins are selected without the first one being replaced. Find $P(\text{quarter, then nickel})$.

8. A coin purse contains 10 pennies, 5 nickels, 3 dimes, and 2 quarters. Two coins are selected without the first one being replaced. Find $P(\text{nickel, then nickel})$.

9. Two dice are rolled. Find the probability that a multiple of three is rolled on one die and an even number is rolled on the second die.

13-5 Study Guide

Permutations

An arrangement or listing in which order is important is called a **permutation**.

Example 1   **There are 6 sailboats in a race. How many arrangements of first, second, and third place are possible?**

There are 6 choices for first place, then 5 choices for second place, then 4 choices for third place.

$6 \times 5 \times 4 = 120$

The number of permutations is 120.

Some arrangements involve all of the members of a group.

Example 2   **There are 6 sailboats in a race. In how many ways can they finish the race?**

There are 6 choices for first, 5 choices for second, and so on.

$6 \times 5 \times 4 \times 3 \times 2 \times 1 = 720$

There are 720 ways in which the sailboats can finish the race.

The expression $6 \times 5 \times 4 \times 3 \times 2 \times 1$ can be written 6!. It is read "six **factorial**." In general, $n!$ is the product of the counting numbers starting at n and counting backward to 1.

Find the value of each expression.

1. 1!

2. 4!

3. $P(5, 2)$

4. $P(7, 3)$

5. In how many ways can winner, first runner-up and second runner-up be chosen from 8 riders in a horse show?

6. In how many ways can 5 horses in a race cross the finish line?

7. In how many different ways can 4 people stand in line for a movie?

8. In how many ways can the gold, silver, and bronze metals be awarded to 10 swimmers?

13-5 Practice

Permutations

Find the value of each expression.

1. 6!

2. 9!

3. $P(6, 3)$

4. $P(9, 8)$

5. $P(10, 1)$

6. $P(8, 8)$

Solve.

7. How many different ways can seven people be seated in one row of seven people?

8. Suppose that eight students out of ten qualify for the cheerleading squad. In how many ways can you choose the squad?

9. In how many ways can a president, vice-president, secretary, and treasurer be chosen from a club with 12 members?

10. In how many ways can five books be arranged on a shelf?

11. In how many ways can a phone number be created if there are ten ways that the first three digits can be arranged and then each of the remaining four digits can be any digit from 0-9 as long as no digit is repeated in the group of four?

12. How many different four-letter words can be made from the alphabet if the first two letters come from the first half of the alphabet and the second two letters come from the second half of the alphabet?

13-6 Study Guide

Combinations

Arrangements or listings in which order is not important are called **combinations**.

Example **In how many ways can 3 toppings for a pizza be chosen from a list of 10 toppings?**

There are $10 \cdot 9 \cdot 8$ permutations of three toppings chosen from ten.

There are 3! or $3 \cdot 2 \cdot 1$ ways to arrange the three toppings.

$$\frac{10 \cdot 9 \cdot 8}{3 \cdot 2 \cdot 1} = \frac{720}{6}$$
$$= 120$$

There are 120 ways that 3 toppings can be chosen.

Solve.

1. In how many ways can 3 representatives be chosen from a group of 11 people?

2. For an English exam, students are asked to write essays on 4 topics from a list of 8 topics. How many different combinations are possible?

3. In how many ways can a 5-player team be chosen from 16 people?

4. In how many different ways can 8 different colors for a crayon box be selected from 24 color choices?

13-6 **Practice**

Combinations

Solve.

1. How many different ways can five out of seven team members be chosen for the basketball team if order is not important?

2. List all combinations of Roshanda, Shelli, Toshi, and Hector, taken three at a time.

3. At Heavenly Ice Cream, customers may choose three of the following toppings to make an ice cream sundae.

   peanut butter chips, chocolate chips, coconut, chopped nuts, granola, sliced strawberries, fudge sauce, caramel sauce

   If it is equally likely that a customer will choose any combination of three toppings, find the probability that a customer will choose sliced strawberries, caramel sauce, and coconut or peanut butter chips, coconut, and fudge sauce.

4. In the Illinois State Lottery, balls are numbered from 1 to 54 and put into a machine, which scrambles them. Six balls are then selected in any order. How many different ways can the winning number be chosen?

Mathematics: Applications and Connections, Course 2